The Great Walks of Dartmoor

Terry Bound

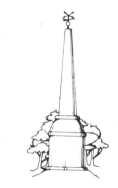

OBELISK PUBLICATIONS

OTHER DARTMOOR TITLES FROM OBELISK PUBLICATIONS

The A to Z of Dartmoor Tors, Terry Bound
Diary of a Dartmoor Walker, Chips Barber
Diary of a Devonshire Walker, Chips Barber
Under Sail thr S Devon & Dartmoor, R.B. Cattell
The Great Little Dartmoor Book, Chips Barber
Dartmoor in Colour, Chips Barber
Ten Family Walks on Dartmoor, Sally & Chips Barber
Dark & Dastardly Dartmoor, Sally & Chips Barber
Weird & Wonderful Dartmoor, Sally & Chips Barber
The Templer Way, Derek Beavis
Tales of the Teign, Chips Barber & Judy Chard

*For further details of these or any of our titles, please send SAE to
Obelisk Publications at the address below, or telephone Exeter (0392) 68556*

For Hazel

PLATE ACKNOWLEDGEMENTS

Jeremy Wellens for pages 40, 55, 95. Terry Bound for pages 8, 24, 25, 72. R.W.J. Norton for pages 35, 48, 53, 54, 76, 82, 94, 97, 108, 111. Steve Cox for pages 61, 102. Express & Echo (Bert Davies) for page 107. Chips Barber for pages 4, 12, 17, 32, 51, 68, 70, 81, 99, 100, 109, 110. Cover illustration taken by Chips Barber in the Tavy Cleave. All drawings by Jane Reynolds. Dave Whalley for all maps

N.B. It is inevitable that since this book was first published, some changes should have taken place on Dartmoor. Because of declining numbers, the North-South Walk is no longer an annual event; the official walk was last held in June 1990. In any case, recent decisions taken by the Dartmoor National Park Committee recommend that notice is given of proposed events similar to the type described in this book. Serious erosion problems were envisaged and the DNP are anxious to keep their fingers on the pulse of leisure activities on the moor.
For Walk 7 the parking arrangements have changed and parking places are now provided a little way up the lane from the Dartmoor Inn, on the right hand side. A stile leads to open moorland. The Cornwall and Devon group of the LDWA is again organising the annual 100-mile walk in 1994. A small part of the 1984 route will be used, but as the next walk will be anti-clockwise, these instructions will not be of use. However, if you wish to follow in their footsteps, this 100 mile walk should provide an enjoyable romp around another of the Great Walks of Dartmoor. On page 31, line 21, for Sinder Park read Snider Park and on line 33, it is the Lich Way and not the Mariners' Way; on page 88, line 34, please read Erme Pound and not pond!

*First published in 1985
Reprinted in 1992
by Obelisk Publications, 2 Church Hill, Pinhoe, Exeter, Devon,
Designed, typeset and printed in Great Britain
by Penwell Print Ltd, Kelly Bray, Callington, Cornwall*

CONTENTS

Enthusiastic letterboxers at Ducks' Pool on Southern Dartmoor

Preface

"Oh no, not *another* book on Dartmoor!" will be the cry. Yes, but this one's a bit different. Archaeology, topography, geology, botany and zoology have all been more than adequately studied and recorded in other publications. This book, while appreciating the work of past experts, is aimed at the walker who likes both walking and the moor.

The output of books concerning Dartmoor must have doubled in the last five or six years with the accent on walking—none yet has included all the organised walks. Some authors have based the time or distance of the walk on the availability of a car, horse, bus route or pub but I shall only involve that slightly longer walk which the real moor enthusiast can undertake; it can be regarded as the next step in a progression from a six-to-ten-mile walk, found elsewhere, to the all-day challenge in completing a longer form of exercise.

With planning, some of the journeys may be divided into two parts depending on the fitness of the participants—a natural break, maybe. I have, whenever possible, given grid-references of salient spots. On most of the organised events you can make your own way from one checkpoint to the next—in most cases the route is obvious. However, should you attempt any of these walks, plan in advance and tell someone reliable of your objective, for your own sake. Dartmoor weather changes with little or no warning, sometimes dramatically, and it *does* help to be aware that others know of your intentions. So be prepared—remind yourself of the correct procedures in unfavourable circumstances. For example, walk in a group so that emergency equipment may be shared between you—a kit check is obligatory on the "challenge" walks.

My own experiences have taught me the following:

1. If completely lost, walk downhill. One disadvantage is that you may be walking away from your destination, but you will eventually find some civilisation which you can recognise from the map, e.g. a tinners' hut, a 180° bend in the river, or, better still, a bridge. You may also find boggy areas but they can be skirted while keeping the river in view.

2. On warmer days, take more than enough liquid. Squash, refrigerated overnight and poured into a vacuum flask, is an ideal drink, especially when devoured with succulent food such as a jelly slab or

5

fruit sweets. Personally, I prefer jam sandwiches to meat, cheese or crusty rolls, being more moist and easier to chew, and besides, eating a little at each short stop is better than a full-scale picnic every two or three hours.

3. Trust your compass; whenever I have failed to use it, I have had reason to regret it.

It is assumed, I hope with confidence, that the reader who intends to follow the routes will have knowledge of map-reading, of some historical background to the sites, and will have some idea of walkers' etiquette.

The walks in this book have been described mainly for pleasure but partly as a challenge. Don't try to complete all the walks in one day—or even a week. If you are not used to using your legs day in, day out, or if you drive to work and back each day, even if you are physically drained after reading half of this book, then prepare yourself gradually. Build up to a four-, six-, eight-, ten-miles a day stroll over a period of weeks rather than days. Give after-effects a chance to do their worst, and then if they do, use your legs around the home, office, factory etc. to shake off any aches. This, I found, is better than lying or sitting around for two or three days. Take care of your muscles. They have feelings, not emotions perhaps, but senses. Therefore, respect them. You will know how they feel if you can walk twelve-to-twenty miles in a day already with no serious repercussions. But walk a little further each time, not over-exerting your body's capacity for exercise but realising when you reach it.

This book is dedicated to the mentally enthusiastic who are physically prepared. Happy walking!

1

The Abbot's Way

Historical Background

In medieval times, religious houses sprang up in many places all over Britain. The "Age of Learning" was yet to come but the middle classes endeavoured to maintain a comparatively civilised way of life—not utterly wanting to become nobles or even squires of the landed gentry but having enough wit about them to keep what they had and gradually improve their lot. Girls were sent to work at the manor and were expected to either marry merchants or farmers. Boys were apprenticed to learn a trade from friends of the family or in the nearest town. The lucky ones were taught to read, write and to think for themselves—education was a hit-or-miss affair in those days, outside the monasteries. So it was to the monks that the youths were sent: to learn, to be disciplined and to act in a Christian way and to continue that life-style when they returned home.

Among the abbeys in Devon, Buckfast remains the most famous, probably because it is a modern building—large, airy and most attractive in design—and possibly because the Benedictine Order has a worldly commercialism in producing wines and honey. Completed between the wars, Buckfast Abbey stands on the site of a far older establishment which may not have sold wine and honey, but offered manna in a spiritual way to many passers-by. Situated just off the modern trunk road, A38 between Ashburton and Buckfast-leigh, this Abbey has a counterpart on the other side, the west, of the moor.

Buckland Abbey, once owned by Sir Francis Drake and now in the hands of the National Trust, is as historically important as Buckfast. While Buckfast was founded by the King of Wessex in 790, Buckland's noble connections began with its founding by Amicia, Countess of Devon in 1280. The land surrounding the abbey stretched, according to the Countess' charter, as far as the boundary of the Forest at Nun's Cross, South and North Hessary Tors and Great Mis Tor (see the Perambulation Walk).

It is reasonable to suggest that the brethren at both abbeys and the tradespeople of the respective neighbourhoods had enough in common to establish physical links with each other, and a track be-

tween the villages would be followed many times a year. So often, in fact, that what could be called "The Abbot's Way" can be traced on the ground. There is some disagreement among historians as to what constitutes the path from Buckfast to Buckland, and what is termed the "Jobbers' Path". William Crossing states that the latter is the Abbot's Way; Robert Groves concludes that traders would be more likely to use the more direct route. Hansford Worth, while agreeing partially with Groves, adds that the Abbots followed crosses over the moor, many of which are standing today. It is

A Kit Check before the Abbot's Way Walk

unlikely, then, that many people would have followed the exact route which the organisers of the walk lay down. A link from the northern route to Tavistock, via Holne Moor, follows the Forest Boundary from Broad Rock to Nun's Cross to North Hessary Tor, near which it meets yet another probable track. This is followed by tracing the line of several stones inscribed with 'T' and 'A', assumedly Tavistock and Ashburton. Again it is questionable whether the monks from Tavistock Abbey, founded in 961, would have had these guide-stones to follow, or whether they led over the quickest, or more direct, less marshy way.

The Abbot's Way walk itself veers away from the traditional path *at Broad Rock (Grid Reference 618672). The easier terrain which leads to Buckland crosses the River Plym at Plym Steps (GR 603672) and cuts across Ditsworthy Warren meeting the Eylesbarrow Mine track. It then passes Ringmoor Cottage (GR 558666) and bears right to follow a wall downhill to Marchant's Cross. This is another bondmark of the Buckland Abbey estates and stands where this branch of the Abbot's Way crosses a track from Tavistock Abbey to Plympton Priory.*

The Abbot's Way walk, organised by the Tavistock and District Youth and Community Services Committee, takes place on the first Sunday in October. The day starts with a kit-check at Buckfast Abbey. (That is, in the grounds, not in the vestry!) Given the all-clear, if you mean to take part in The Event and on The Day, you leave the Abbey grounds, turn right, then soon, left (i.e. west) and ahead for the next half-mile. Turn right, then left and in another quarter-mile turn right, then left again. Continue along this road for about two miles, arriving at a T-junction of the road, and you are on the edge of the moor, at Cross Furzes. A way-marked track leads downhill toward the Dean Burn which is crossed by both a foot-bridge and a ford. Bear right going up the other bank and follow a narrow, worn path marked by poles, bearing south of west before dropping down steeply to cross another stream. The path takes a sweep around the northern edge of Grippers Hill, passing through a gate and eventually aiming for a pole used as a guide post on the brow of the hill. If you are lucky, most of this stretch of path from Cross Furzes is marked by orange blobs. (If you're unlucky, the paint will have worn off.)

A marvellous view can be had from this point. Ahead lies the little valley of the Brockhill Stream, running into the Avon Reservoir. Behind this are the cairn-topped Eastern and Western White Barrows, nearly a mile apart. The former is the one similar in shape to a submarine. Across the Brockhill valley is Dean Moor and behind that, another hill crowned with a cairn: this is Huntingdon Warren topped by the "Heap of Sinners". To the right, and in the distance, lies a faint track leading to Puper's Rocks.

Few of the participants on the Walk itself give enough time to take in the view—if it's raining or misty there *is* no view—but they surge on down to Brockhill Ford and bear slightly left to skirt around Dean Moor on the Reservoir side. For the next mile or so the track appears to be more worn than before, possibly because many people, leaving their cars at Shipley Bridge (further down the Avon), walk up one side of the river, perambulate the reservoir and go down the opposite side. A good view up the Avon Valley above the reservoir comes into sight as the direction veers to north of west. The next stream, Western Walla Brook enters the Avon at the south-east corner of Huntingdon Warren; here stands Huntingdon Cross. This emblem was said to have been erected by the trans-moor monks themselves as a guide, but the lie of the land in this area would imply that the easiest route would follow the river upstream anyway and no guide would be necessary. The cross was also intended to be a bond mark for the lands of Sir William Petre where his manor touched the Forest of Dartmoor proper—see the Perambulation walk.

Continuing due west, and following the same well-trodden path, it becomes clear that the Avon will soon change direction and run from the north. On the opposite bank a small tributary foots a wide and shallow valley and it is at this point, Buckland Ford, (660662) that the Way itself crossed the Avon. Although this river appears wide but shallow at this point, it may be best to stay on the north bank for a while. Even after little rain, some Dartmoor rivers can be forded only with difficulty, or with ill-chosen expletives, or both. To follow the river for another 300 yards has an advantage and a slight disadvantage. The good news is the clapper bridge which gives a dry crossing; the bad news is the steep slope you have to negotiate almost at once. Tracing the original route followed by the abbots, from Buckland Ford, becomes difficult: the best way is to follow the shallow valley, previously mentioned, south for a few hundred paces, until a deep gully is seen on your right—to the west. Follow this to its head, climbing up the floor of the gully, then aim for the brow of the hill, walking due west. If the Avon is crossed by clapper, the steeper slope is encountered. A compass bearing of 260° from the clapper can be taken, or one of 250° from the top of the hill. Whichever of these two options is taken, the motorway of the south moor will be met, running at this point north-south. This is the track of the Redlake Railway, the seven mile long route from Bittaford, near Ivybridge, to the china-clay works. The conical pile to your right is only one of the remains of a once-flourishing industry. Depending on your compass bearing, you will walk a few more yards south along the track until it bends to the west. Those following the "gully" route above Buckland Ford, should see the track below and to the right. In all three instances, pause where this track meets a less obvious, but clearly-defined, track leaving this at an angle of 30° near a ruined building, a few paces to the right. You are now at Crossways (647659) having completed one-third of the journey.

From here, follow the path to the right, downhill at an angle towards the stream, also on your right. In less than half a mile a prominent boundary stone appears to the left of your path (uphill) about 40 yards away. This is one of several stones striding across the moor from the south marking the boundary between Ugborough and Harford parishes. The two most northerly can be seen from the track, that is the one mentioned above, and the other is on the bank of the Redlake on the right. The latter is called the "Outer U stone" as it has inscribed on it the initial letter of the parish of Ugborough.

Soon the Abbot's Way crosses this stream at a small ford, but there are many boulders affording a choice of crossing. A faint path can be followed on the north bank of the stream, contouring around Green Hill to and from Dry Lake Ford (634664) as far as Blacklane Brook and to the head of the River Erme, reached in half a mile after the Brook. Here are several remains of tinners' activities—blowing-house ruins, rubble mounds, gullies—typical of this area of the moor. The next point to aim for is a rock! In less than half a mile from Erme Head and proceeding in the same direction (north-west) Broad Rock stands, or rather lies, beyond an area of scattered rocks just before the watershed of the Plym and Erme. It is less than 3 feet high but is 12 feet long and nearly 6 feet wide with the initials "BB" inscribed on it (standing for Blatchford Boundary, the northern extent of the manor of the Blatchford family, late of Cornwood). The grid reference is 618672 and it is at this point that the branch to Buckland Abbey diverges. A compass bearing (330°) can be followed to Plym Ford but it is possible to contour Great Gnats Head as shown on the 1:25000 OS map of Buckfastleigh. This shows a path leading towards the ford but there is little trace of a track or path in this immediate vicinity. However, Plym Ford is an obvious crossing place and it is advisable to follow one of the gullies leading from it, going north from the Ford to walk slightly west of north to the brow of the hill.

From here another fine view can be had with many tors and hills spread around in a semi-circle, all seemingly watching over each others' shoulders at you as you go. Ahead lies Foxtor Mires with the

Nun's Cross Farm—Bed & Breakfast with a difference!

black-washed houses of Whiteworks behind. To the right of these are a few trees and two grey buildings. It is to these that you should now proceed. As you do so look to your left occasionally to notice on the next rise a track also heading toward the same buildings. These are what remains of Nun's Cross Farm. Recently, there have been attempts to render the newer building habitable for youth groups and adventure training schemes. Behind the farm, and visible behind a bank to the west, stands Nun's Cross itself, one of the largest naturally-hewn crosses of the moor (see Widgery Cross, under The Memorial Walk).

The next part of the Abbot's Way walk follows the border of the Forest (see the Perambulation Walk) where it touches the lands formerly belonging to Buckland Abbey as part of the gift of Amicia, Countess of Devon, in 1280. The way is easily followed as the track has been used by vehicles for part of the way from the farm towards Castle Lane, the road from Princetown to Whiteworks. In three-quarters of a mile the track veers right but the path continues ahead, undulating but gradually rising, to South Hessary Tor (formerly known as Look-out Tor by Princetonians). A number of boundary stones have been passed since Nun's Cross, some of which are inscribed "PCWW". These indicate the catchment area of Burrator Reservoir; other stones are set into the enclosure wall on the right of the path.

The direction suggested by the organisers of the Walk takes the participant in a nearly straight line to North Hessary Tor, but a diversion may be made for various reasons into Princetown by following the wall for another mile. I mention this because it is unlikely that monks would climb unnecessarily and instead (if they ever did come *this* way from Buckfast) would have come quite close to the present-day foundations of the Princetown Railway. In all events, the next indication in this area that any religious orders ever tramped over the moor is Windy Post (534743), three miles away.

The easiest route to take from North Hessary Tor is to walk north west towards Hollow Tor and head for the group of trees three quarters of a mile away at the side of the road. This was originally the site of a school attended by the children of the quarrymen who worked at the numerous quarries in the vicinity—"Four Winds" is the appropriate name of this site. Follow the road down to Merrivale Bridge and up Pork Hill until you pass the milestone on the north side of the road. Almost due south is the prominent pile of Vixen Tor, the tallest but not the highest rocks on the moor. To the right, and in the middle distance, is Feather Tor, a much lower pile, and slightly to the right again you may just make out Windy Post. Walk towards this cross, or towards Feather Tor (bearing 230°) until Windy Post is visible (534743). There you will find the Grimstone and Sortridge leat.

Walk downhill with the gully on your right and the path becomes a track. In half a mile you will meet a right-angled road at the entrance to Moortown Farm. Walk ahead (west) along the road for three quarters of a mile and at the top of a short rise, at a T-junction, go ahead, bearing slightly right at the fork of two paths. (Beware of flying balls!) As your path levels, you can pick out, almost straight ahead, "The Pimple", a strange pepper-pot building perched on a mound about a mile away. Don't walk directly towards it, but cross the metalled road at an acute angle to aim for a boundary post, where your next destination should be the junction of road and

13

track at the Tavistock Golf Club's Clubhouse.

Unfortunately, but necessarily, the rest of the walk follows roads to the end, and unless you use grass verges, you may find the pavements of Tavistock a bit of a let-down after the springy turf of the golf course. Follow the road downhill for half a mile turning left at the main road, then right at the pub, passing under the track of the Tavistock-Yelverton branch of the former Plym Valley line. Bear left at the river with the park in front of you and at the A386 Plymouth road, turn right to cross West Bridge. The school on your left is your ultimate goal although you may also pass through those on the hockey pitches, enjoying your last stretch of turf. The remains of Tavistock Abbey are half a mile away towards the town centre at the other end of the park, and opposite the Bedford Hotel.

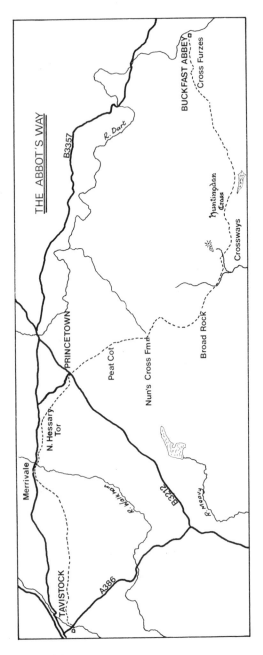

14

ITINERARY

Checkpoints	Approx Time	Accumulative Distance km	(miles)	Grid Refs
Buckfast	9.00			741674
Cross Furzes	9.45	4.5	(2.5)	700667
Huntingdon Cross	10.35	8.5	(5.0)	665662
Crossways	11.40	11.5	(7.0)	647659
Broad Rock	12.00	15.0	(9.5)	618672
Peat Cot	12.55	19.5	(12.5)	603710
(Princetown—edge of)	1.40	22.5	(14.0)	587733
North Hessary Tor	2.00	23.75	(15.0)	578743
Merrivale	2.40	26.75	(17.5)	550751
(Tavistock GC Club House)	4.05	33.0	(22.0)	493737
Tavistock School	4.30	35.0	(23.5)	476737

Total time taken out for stops: 1 hour

2

The Lich Way

Historical Background

Most people have seen or heard of a lich-gate, a thatched or tiled entrance to a churchyard, which was the penultimate resting place of the departed before the service and burial. The Lich Way or Path on Dartmoor is therefore not where the dead walk but a route along which they were taken to their parish church, in a coffin!

Since the time when it was ordained that all except suicides shall be buried at the parish church, men have experienced events which, for good or bad reasons, have filled many a book. The Forest of Dartmoor lies wholly within the parish of Lydford—the parish of Lydford is made up almost completely of the Forest of Dartmoor—and up to 1260 the deceased, of farms and villages from up to sixteen moorland miles away, would be accompanied by relatives and friends on the day of their funeral. No shiny black limousines for them—unless they called shire horses limousines. Instead, the body would have had to be borne from the place of residence to the parish churchyard.

There were complaints. Inhabitants of the tenements in the East Dart and Walla Brook valleys suggested to Bishop Bronescombe of Exeter that Widecombe Church was only half the distance of that to Lydford. The Bishop put down his cheese butty and gave dispensation for the residents of Pizwell (668785) and Babeny (672752) to bury their dead at Widecombe. No doubt these two tenements and Runnage, Riddon and Brimpts, being in Walla Brook valley, all took advantage of His Grace's benefaction. The notorious Coffin Stones on Dartmeet Hill may bear witness, as well as coffins and inscribed initials, to the fact that the bearers could rest their load across the stones while they quenched their thirst with ale before trudging up the hill towards Widecombe.

The other ancient tenements in the East and West Dart Valleys were not so fortunate. The parish boundary whicn follows the Walla Brook to Dartmeet, pushed on to the south over Holne Moor and so included the farms at Sherberton, Dunnabridge, Prince Hall and Huccaby to name but a few. Those to the north of Postbridge on the East Dart had their own way of going to Lydford. The Lich Way,

16

therefore, had many alternative variations and even the route which was most traversed was not the only one!

Experts have found it difficult to trace; some farming methods have obliterated the former route where it passed through or across valleys and even Hansford Worth and Crossing each suggest alternatives. The route we follow is therefore a compromise, but try if you can to imagine an easier or quicker course when you have to carry a corpse and its heavy wooden overcoat.

Beginning at the remains of Bellever clapper bridge (658774) walk west towards the hamlet passing the Youth Hostel and entering the forest. The Lich Way is signposted through the conifers, so there is

The highly volatile Powder Mills

little need to explain the direction. However, the break in the plantation on Lakehead Hill may give you the opportunity to look at a burial chamber a hundred yards to the right and about ten yards inside the forest. It is not completely surrounded by trees, but don't follow the OS map 1:25000 (Two Bridges) as there it is shown to be some way outside the forest (644773). Continue to follow the track through the forest, as many four-wheel-drive vehicles have done, until you regain fresh air and join the Postbridge—Two Bridges road at Cherrybrook Bridge (634770). The guidepost suggests that the route now lies due west but in most months of the year the ground here is extremely wet and in an unsatisfactory state for the first part of a day-long walk. The post points vaguely towards a

17

clapper bridge between you and the disused Powdermills and their chimneys, but I have found the occupants of the neighbouring cottages to be unreliable when it comes to rights of way. It is advisable to walk along the road to the left (south-west) to the first gate on your right, after the track which leads to the same cottages. You may be shouted at, but at least you will be too far away to hear and you will also have skirted the marsh.

Walk uphill at an angle towards the left-hand hill and the scattered piles of Littaford Tor. As you climb, a wall and a gate come into view; head for the gate and towards Longford Tor, the more prominent pile in a conical shape. Go through the gate and cross the ridge between the two named Tors. Ahead of you is the West Dart valley with Wistman's Wood, of Nature Reserve Fame; walk north-west so that you descend at an angle and you make towards the easiest crossing-places of the river. The obvious one is at the weir (608779) but given reasonable conditions many natural rocks in the river can be used.

Once across, walk towards the col between Beardown Hill and Lydford Tor. William Crossing suggests that the latter does not take its name from the parish or the town but alludes to the last syllable in Littaford and Longford, making the observation that it is the Celtic word fford, meaning a track or passage. Passing Lydford Tor, you may be able to discern a faint, worn path which gradually leads towards the wall approaching from your right. Three-quarters of the way down it meets a gate, through which you pass, and taking a bearing of half a right angle from the wall, walk slightly downhill and north-west to meet a well-worn gully. It leads in turn to the Cowsic River, just above the confluence with the stream approaching from the west (Conies Down Stream), at the crossing place called "Travellers' Ford" (592786).

Crossing the Cowsic, keep Conies Down Stream on the left and walk parallel to it keeping 25-30 yards away from it. In this way you will both avoid unnecessary dips and gullies in the banks and will be able to follow one of several narrow paths leading, at about 280°, to the dip in the land between Conies Down on your right and Dunghill. Nearer the watershed, a small patch of gravel will be encountered; walk across it and bear slightly right to find another path leading in the same direction. At the ridge, several narrow tracks appear again and on the horizon ahead a small bump on a slope heralds your next point on the path.

18

Almost in line with it is the ford over the River Walkham. This lies slightly to the right of a straight line and it should not be too difficult to find one of several wider paths to walk to the ford. Follow the dip in between two small steep banks to the right, then bear left, then right again as you ascend. Soon the "bump" appears as a tumulus ahead of you: this is White Barrow, one of the landmarks on the 1240 perambulation. Keep on the track as you approach White Barrow, but on reaching the tumulus bear north-west to gain the firm ground to the other side of the marsh now on your right. Keep walking north-west and within a few hundred yards look for a wall climbing up the slope from your left. Walk towards the 600 yard wide gap between this wall and the corner of the wall under Lynch Tor—the small piles of rocks on the hill-top to your right, half a mile away.

As the walls narrow continue towards the gate and dark green army hut ahead, passing a sign prohibiting service vehicles. This drift lane ends at this hut and gate but many vehicles have worn the path away to a gravel track which you follow to the moorgate, half a mile from the hut. Don't go left through this gate but keep north-west to find a finger-post pointing downhill between two higher walls. Not too many instructions are required for the rest of the walk. Unless you are colour blind with a yellow deficiency, you can enjoy the change of scenery from open moor to idyllic, partially-wooded valleys by following the yellow dots.

A mile from the moorgate, you cross the Baggator Brook and the River Tavy, at Cataloo Steps, the latter fording requiring more care than usual. If it is impossible to cross here, walk north with the Tavy on your left, crossing two walls and in half a mile find a foot-bridge which takes you to an unmade road. This you will meet if you cross the Tavy at Cataloo, turn right over the planks and stile, skirt four fields, cross a fifth and enter the lane. The more northerly crossing (by bridge) was more exciting in the past as large stepping-stones were used—they were wide enough for the coffin bearers to cross the Tavy without changing position. (You forgot you were still supposed to be carrying it, didn't you?) Turn north-east onto the lane and, on meeting the road at Willsworthy, turn left, and soon turn right into another marked footpath at the side of the Wills-worthy Brook (533816). In about 300 yards, a gate bars the way ahead but the Lich Path crosses the stile on the left, the brook, and then bears right to cross another stile before entering open moor-

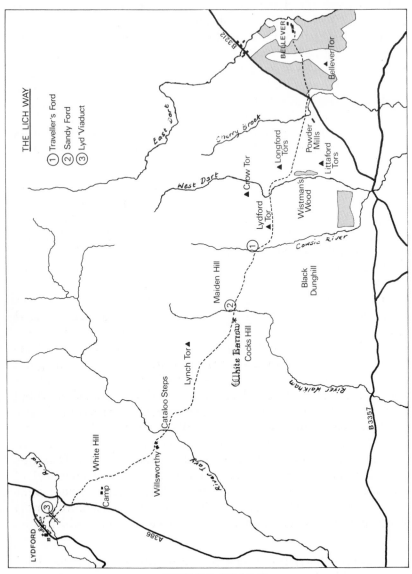

THE LICH WAY

① Traveller's Ford
② Sandy Ford
③ Lyd Viaduct

NOT TO SCALE

20

land again. Follow the edge of the common with the fence on your right and soon, ahead and just to the left, on the near horizon, a shed comes into view (527827). Walk up to it bearing NNW. This hut stands on the bank of the Mine Leat. Cross at the stone bridge and continue along the left bank until it bends to the east fairly sharply, about 250 yards past the hut. From this point, walk on a bearing of 340° to cross another leat and, on the ridge, the military road. Walking to the right of the nissen huts, make for the 15 feet high stone chimney which is almost due north of them. Bear slightly to the left to walk along the top of the east (right) bank of the shallow valley and, after 350 yards, near a range notice board enter a lane via a gate.

This will lead you to the A386 Tavistock—Okehampton road into which you turn right. Just after the house called Beardon, notice the legend on the concrete silo, the "Take-Off Stone" (the first strip-joint in Devon!) and the milestone, all on the left-hand side of the road. The Take-Off Stone was where a team of three horses was reduced to two by the ostler who "took off" a horse so that the other two, having been charged at the toll-gate, could continue. The mile-stone is inscribed: Tavistock 7, Okehampton 8, Truro 57; one assumes that city was the next important town on a once well-used route. The milestone in fact stands on the former main road, now a track, which was part of the King Wall (or Way) which led from Oke-hampton to Meldon to Lake Down to Southerly Down, joining the present line at the Dartmoor Inn, and forming the base of the present road to Tavistock. Walk past the MS on the track downhill for a few paces and turn left to pass through a farmyard. Again, follow the yellow dots, crossing a small stream by a plank and, at a gate, the River Lyd by a more substantial footbridge. Pass in front of a modernised house, under the viaduct and, 270 yards from this structure, turn left at a crossing of tracks and roads. This branch of the four becomes metalled as it passes the cottages on your right and then more dwellings on the left. Turn left into Lydford's main street and, in 250 yards, approach the towered church which is on your right.

It is improbable that wayfarers carrying coffins (and wet handker-chiefs) would follow this last part of their journey exactly, because so much building, enclosing and occupation by the services has necessitated deviations. But, in case you become bereaved in

Bellever or widowed at Wistman's Wood, you are now acquainted with your predecessor's route.

Lydford—the end of the trail!

ITINERARY

	Approx Time	Accumulative Distance		Grid Refs
		km	(miles)	
Bellever (R. Dart)	10.15			658774
Cherrybrook Br	11.00	3.25	(2.0)	634770
Travellers Ford	12.15	8.25	(5.0)	591786
White Barrow	1.15	11.5	(7.0)	568793
Baggator Moorgate	1.45	14.5	(9.0)	547805
Cataloo Steps	2.30	15.5	(9.75)	540811
Willsworthy (Brook Br)	2.50	16.5	(10.5)	533817
Willsworthy Camp	3.15	18.5	(12.0)	524833
Lydford Church	4.00	21.5	(14.5)	509848

3

The North—South Walk

Background Information

Unlike the first two walks, this all-day journey has no obvious historical background. William Crossing (yes, him again) is said to have walked from South Brent to Lydford, and from Okehampton to Ivybridge, in daylight more than once. I, for one, was amazed at his efforts until I tried it for myself.

This, as is the Abbots' Way, is an annual event organised by the Tavistock and District Youth and Community Services Committee.

There are checkpoints, but how you get from A to B is your choice and there are few sheeptracks, paths, lanes or "motorways" to follow for the first two-thirds of the route. I therefore suggest the quicker, but not always easier, way and allow you to see the time we took between the checkpoints. Being North—South, it's all downhill!

From the starting point, at the Observation Post on Okement Hill (602877), walk due south for just over one and a half miles until Fur Tor appears slightly to the right. (Cut Hill, the slightly-domed horizon, is due south; Fur Tor, the group of rock-piles to the right (west) of it.) A small valley develops on your right, and this gives you a good guide. The terrain may be sticky and pitted in places until you reach the brook, but as you proceed it becomes firmer. Keeping the rock-piles ahead of you, pass over the ridge between that stream, the Black Ridge Brook, and the next, Cut Combe Water. Both should present little difficulty in fording, but the slope up to Fur Tor (588831) is steep and a five minute break is welcome.

From here, walk south east (135°) for about a mile until a shallow valley appears to your right. This is the infant Tavy and this you follow until it runs away westwards—to the right. You should continue southwards for another three quarters of a mile when another valley forms ahead. Bear slightly left so that you keep above the east bank and then keep the same height so that you find yourself on the ridge—the river in a steepening valley on your right, and a very tall standing-stone ahead. This is Beardown Man (Celtic 'maen' = stone) GR 595795; Devil's Tor is a few yards away to the east.

Keeping on the ridge between the Cowsic to the west and the West Dart to the east you walk over moderately easy ground to Lydford Tor (599781), one mile away, then bear left to follow one of three gullies to the river (608779) on the Dart. Cross it and follow the valley south, keeping Wistman's Wood to your right, avoiding both unnecessary damage to the Nature Reserve and several areas of ill-drained turf. A few walls are encountered which are crossed by stiles or gates, all of which are denoted by orange-painted discs. This will lead you past Crockern Farm and along the farm track to Two Bridges (608750).

The next stretch is unique in that the owner of Roundhill Farm

Fur Tor—Dartmoor's most remote tor

only allows right of way across his land once a year—when the North—South walk takes place. The route from Two Bridges takes the Princetown road for 300 yards and enters the drive on the left, past Roundhill Cottages, to the farm. Walk down through marked gates to the wooden bridge over the Blackbrook River and through the gate in the next wall (uphill and to the left) and continue over Royal Hill for two miles, passing the valley of the Strane on your right and the tumulus (608719) on your left (bearing from the last gate, 150°). Passing through yet another gate, cross the Swincombe twice and make your way towards the cross based on a pedestal at a bearing of 160°—this is Childe's Tomb. To "make tracks" too much to the right will take you towards the worst areas of Foxtor Mires,

24

thus you should cross the Swincombe by the hard ground, and walk up the east bank so that you can step over the brook again when convenient to walk to Childe's Tomb (626703).

Your alternative to avoid Roundhill enclosures starts way back at the second wall after Wistman's Wood. Instead of passing through the gate follow the wall to the left for a quarter of a mile passing Parson's Cottage to the north, under Crockern Tor. This will take you through a gate to the B3212 Postbridge—Two Bridges road. Turn left and walk for three-quarters of a mile to turn right onto a waymarked path. In under a mile the Ashburton road is met; here turn right and left towards Moorlands Farm between the avenue of trees. Follow the road for 400 yards bearing left above Prince Hall (625742) and the Youth Training Centre on your left, cross the Dart, bear left and uphill at an angle to the fork in the track. Bear south, using all available gates, keeping the little valley of the Rue Lake on your left. From here, walk west of south for three-quarters of a mile while the larger Swincombe valley appears ahead and to the

Childe the Hunter's tomb

left. Soon, within a few more paces, Childe's Tomb appears (626703). Cross the river and walk along the bank to the monument, crossing when it is safe to do so.

From Childe's Tomb walk up to Fox Tor, walk south avoiding a

25

deep and marshy gully on the left, then up the shallow valley towards the col between Cater's Beam on the east and Crane Hill to the west. A railway sleeper appears, upright like a standing stone— in this case, a standing wood. Continue in the same direction but keep the widening stream on your left and walk along the top of the ridge, so that, in another three-quarters of a mile, the next checkpoint is seen.

Although it is nominally at Ducks' Pool, the Pool itself (627678) with its memorial plaque to William Crossing (yes, the same one!) is to the south-west, 200 yards away. If you now walk south-east for two miles you arrive at the next checkpoint! It's as easy as that apart from some rough ground and some marsh at Dry Lake (Dry? Huh!) After a mile you should be able to walk towards White-barrow, the cairn on the hill in the same direction (south-east).

Alternatively you can follow the Blacklane Brook south from Ducks' Pool to its confluence with the Erme; the Erme to its meeting with the Redlake, just over half a mile away; up the Red-lake to the boundary stones, one on the hillside to the right, the other by the stream on your left; follow the well-worn track uphill and to the south-east to Crossways, the junction of the Abbot's Way (so called) and the wide Redlake railway track (647659). After this—(I said it was easy!) turn right (to the west) and walk along the track for a few paces (about four miles). You have on your right, one of the moor's most attractive and historically most interesting valley, that of the River Erme. The views, on a clear day, are comparatively limited but features on both sides of the valley are noteworthy. A mile down the track the direction veers nearly due west for a short stretch and you may be able to discern a stone circle on the opposite hill. This indicates the southern end of the world's (reputedly) longest stone row, well over two miles from the circle north to Green Hill. Further down the track Left Lake pool (647634) is found among several artificial mounds of spoil tips—the visible remnants of a china-clay enterprise; one on a smaller scale than that at Redlake. In another mile Stalldown Barrow is to the west, while in the distance Shell Top is visible for a time. In the valley lies Piles Copse, one of the three indigenous areas of woodland remaining on the Moor—Wistman's Wood being the only one within the Forest. You pass a prominent rocky hill, Sharp Tor, on your right, the cairn on its summit being less than 300 yards from the track.

Ahead lies Piles Hill (653610) crowned with a low grassy cairn. As the track veers to the east of it, stay to the right and begin the descent towards Harford Moorgate. There are several sheep-tracks which you can follow, and many clues to the local water authority's presence; keep walking south-west and a mile after leaving the track you will arrive at the Moorgate. The square tower of Harford Church is clearly visible from the hill-side —when you are due east of it, walk towards it to the small car park at the gate. Go through the gate, down the lane, turn left at the church and follow this road the rest of the way into Ivybridge.

There is a checkpoint outside Harford Church (638595) which necessitates leaving the moor earlier than an open-air enthusiast might wish. Otherwise, the track could have been followed from Piles Hill past Hanger-shell Rock (a short square pile to the left of the track) curving to the left around Weatherdon Hill with its cairns and then angling off to the right towards the corner of enclosure walls. A gate faces you, (100 yards to the left of the angle) through which you pass into a green

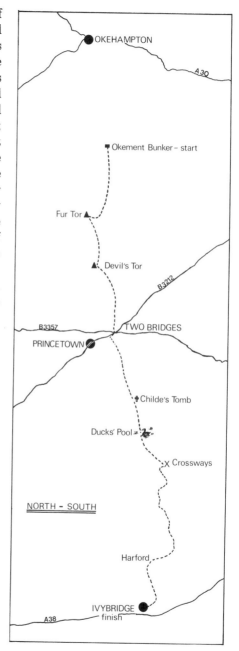

lane which in turn takes you to the Harford road in about half a mile. The official route along the lane from Harford meets this alternative near Stowford House, on your right, and, as you cross the railway, look for one of only four inscribed stones depicting the Two Moors Way. The official walk ends at the Community College just past the bridge, on the left. Independent walkers can continue into the town only 400 yards away, and all down hill!

ITINERARY

Checkpoints	Approx Time	Accumulative Distance km	(miles)	Grid Refs
Okement Hill	9.00			602877
Fur Tor	10.00	5.25	(3.5)	588831
Devil's Tor	10.50	9.25	(6.0)	596796
Two Bridges	12.00	15.25	(9.5)	608750
Childe's Tomb	1.05	21.25	(13.25)	626703
Ducks' Pool	1.50	24.25	(15.0)	628678
Crossways	2.30	27.25	(17.0)	647659
Harford Church	3.45	35.5	(22.0)	638595
Ivybridge CC	4.35	39.0	(24.5)	638566

Time taken out for stops: 50 mins

4

The O.A.T.S. Walk

Background Information

This event is run by the Okehampton and District Youth Centre and is an annual walk from the borders of south Dartmoor to Okehampton, a distance of 27 miles. There is also a half-way walk starting a couple of hours later from Postbridge to end at the same destination, 12 miles distant. (O.A.T.S., by the way, doesn't refer to porridge—or anything else—but to Okehampton Adventure Training Scheme.)

The starting point of the walk was not the start of the walk; unfortunately cars are asked to drop participants at Torr, where the road from Cornwood meets that from Harford (the later stages of walk No. 12, Round the Houses). The continuous uphill walk for about three-quarters of a mile (1 km) to the setting-off point at New Waste (625611) is along a narrow, tree-lined lane. After checking in, the walkers make their own way to the first on-moor checkpoint at Fish Lake.

All follow the left-hand wall going due north, then deviate. Some turn right to follow the waterworks track into the Erme Valley; some go directly uphill almost to the summit of Stall Down; others continue due north to pass over the western slope of that down to bear right slightly, towards "The Dancers", (635644) a stone circle towards which the majority of walkers will be aiming. We chose the middle route, meeting the stone row west of Stalldon Barrow and, keeping the Erme below us to the right, crossed two tributaries of that river before reaching "The Dancers".

From this point, the south end of the longest stone row in Europe, about 2¼ miles (4 km), we followed the stones northward (of course!), crossing the Erme near Erme Pound and, one hour after leaving New Waste, crossed the Redlake. Up to now, the going underfoot had been relatively easy but now, over a more level terrain but badly drained, we had to plough through soft ground and tussocky grass for another mile and a half (2 km). The sight of many colleagues ahead of and behind us gave assurance that we were heading in the right direction. With the shallow valley of the

Avon on our right, and the featureless slopes of Green Hill on the left, this was the most uninteresting and uninspiring part of the day. The only redeeming feature in view was the little group of people clustered around a yellow tent ahead of us, the Fish Lake checkpoint (647682). A few walkers sat in the ruins of the tinners' hut while some, finding the letterbox, signed in for the second time in five minutes. We didn't stop but continued across the stream and, finding a sheep track, carried on walking northwards towards the next checkpoint on Ter Hill.

Although still featureless, the area required careful study if we were to navigate accurately—to the right lay the bog of Avon Mires; ahead, a gently rising slope; to the left, one or two gullies between us and the neighbouring valley, the Swincombe. Keeping north, the slope was traversed and before long, a stone cross appeared slightly to the left. A little to the east of it was the marshals' tent (642707). Here we decided to use our compasses as the clouds were lowering. We wanted a direct line to a gap in the

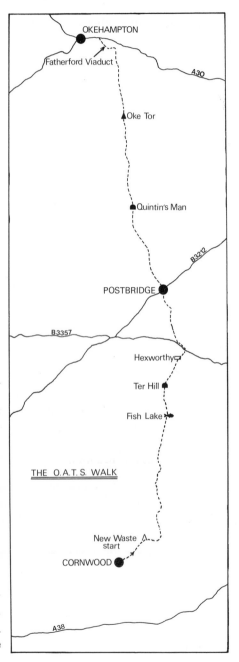

enclosures above Hexworthy and a bearing of 30°, with an estimated distance of two kilometres by map, should see us through. From the top of Ter Hill, we had now a more varied view—Foxtor Mires and Whiteworks to the west and Bellever Tor and the forest around it four miles ahead—we were to have a close-up view of these features later.

Finding the enclave, rather like a very wide driftlane, we walked down to the gate in the right-hand corner and, meeting the lane, turned right then left to drop towards the Forest Inn, *outside* of which the next checkpoint was situated (655726). We had been on the moor for over two hours and decided to have a rest by the war memorial. The sky was now completely overcast and we thought we were in for a wet walk. Only one-third of the walk was completed and walking in the wet for five or six hours is not the best way to spend a Sunday in mid April.

We restarted after ten minutes or so following the road downhill past the famous Jolly Lane Cot, built in one day in 1832, and crossed the West Dart at Huccaby Bridge. Here, the rain began— well, it started as rain but it turned to hail almost at once so we didn't get very wet, but it hurt! By the time we passed St Raphael's Chapel and reached the Ashburton-Tavistock road at Sinder Park Wood, the weather had brightened considerably. Turning left, we headed for Huccaby Cottage where we found the waymarked path across the moor to the north-west. Inscribed "Hucaby Ring" it led along the well trodden path, passed the ring, Huccaby Tor itself and crossed the wall. We next passed Outer Huccaby Ring and headed for the standing stone, prominent between us and the low-ranging rocks of Laughter Tor (652753).

The menhir being on a ridge, we could see our next objective, the corner of the forest in line with Bellever Tor. We crossed the stile in the wall at the forest's edge and turned north along the edge of the forest. We kept in the open for about a mile, until another gate with a nearby signpost was reached. The Mariners' Way was crossed just inside the forest and, still walking north, we were now on a gravelly track. One problem which can be met with in areas such as this is the lack of up-dated maps. The Forestry Commission, which has control of most of the coniferous woodland on Dartmoor, opens up tracks when one area of pine-wood is felled and removed and re-afforested, and previous pathways are left in disrepair. The First

Edition of the 1:25000 series has such tracks marked, and a few acres of recently forested moor is not shown.

After another mile-and-a-bit, we emerged into the daylight opposite the new National Park Information Bureau and shop at Postbridge (646788). Checkpoint No. 4, and a large crowd of walkers, cars, dogs, day-trippers, lunch packs and marshals congregated around the top end of the car park. Here we rested, ate and drank for twenty minutes or so. At this point, the 12 mile walk had set off at ten o'clock, bound for Okehampton. Groups of novice walkers, families, cub-scouts and similar organisations use this exercise as a trial for longer events to come. They, too, receive a certificate on completion.

Setting off for Quintin's Man, we opted, like the majority, to use the west bank of the East Dart leaving Postbridge by Drift Lane, using concrete slabs, wooden stakes and tufts of grass to negotiate the muddy tracts. Again, the path is very well-used—too well-used, some may think—and it follows the wall past the Archerton enclosures on the left and the ancient Broadun (Broad Down) Ring on the slope to the right. The path drops down after half-a-mile or so to a feeder stream of the Dart, and climbs steeply to a stile in a wall at a dry leat. This old water-course leads from the run-off point on the East Dart just below "Dart Turn" and to the west, contours the slope above Archerton to approach the site of the Powder Mills at Cherrybrook.

Here we had another choice: follow the leat and the valley of the Dart and Lade Hill Stream to Grey Wethers, below and east of Sittaford Tor. From here, we would soon be able to see the next checkpoint on the hill on the other side of the Teign. Or, we could climb over Broad Down on a bearing which would lead us to the foot of Winney's Down Brook, follow that combe to the dip to the west of Sittaford Tor and pass the head of Little Varracombe. We chose this latter route chiefly because it was shorter and the energy spent in two climbs would have equalled, in our opinion, that spent on the longer but more level way to the east.

The weather continued to be kind to us and we knew that once Quintin's Man was reached, only one short ascent was left before Okehampton was reached. Therefore, we followed the wall leading

up the hill from the stile to the summit and dropped steeply down to the East Dart, here flowing to the north-east, at the confluence of Winney's Down Brook. We crossed the river without trouble and began the slog up the valley of the brook. It took us twenty minutes or so from the Dart to the point where we first sighted Quintin's Man, just a little west of north. I was waiting for my second (or was it third or fourth) wind, but the terrain was comparable to that at Green Hill—uneven, squelchy and on which it was difficult to maintain a rhythmic pace. But, on sighting the flagpole, the pace picked up—now striding down to the Teign and finding at once that someone had left a few friendly boulders in the river for us to use when crossing. Another burst up the hill to the tent near the cairn and we had completed over two-thirds of the walk. Both of us needed refreshing or, as Crossing would say: "We broke open our wallets and made good use of them". As at previous checkpoints, other groups were already there, standing, talking, eating, drinking and taking in the view; cultivated to the east, desolate to the west.

We restarted after a short but much-needed break and began walking along a faint track toward Whitehouse Hill, which is a maze of peat-passes, pools, peat-hags and piles (of turf). From the hill, and due north, was the flagpole on Hangingstone Hill (617861). A most frequented height for Ten Tor groups this because it is, at the same time, both isolated and easy to reach; this hill has two small buildings erected by the military and a small tor which can be easily missed, as the shelters are built into the rock faces.

Again, we were not alone, but few people seemed to be willing to make a move toward Okehampton. Perhaps they weren't on the OATS walk at all, and were only out for a stroll having their peace shattered by four hundred pedestrians. The rough track, used by the army when they raise the red flag on Hangingstone Hill, led us down to the River Taw. We passed the previous year's checkpoint at the ruins of a recently demolished observation post on the trackside and, after three miles from Quintin's Man and one-and-a-half from Hangingstone, entered Steeperton Gorge near the ruins of Knock Mine (614884). The Taw was low enough to cross on the stones, and we kept to the track leading steeply uphill onto the ridge between the Taw and the East Okement rivers. Ahead lay Oke Tor, the penultimate marshals' post—level going, not so stony and we felt an increasing sense of relief that the difficult part was over.

At Oke Tor (613900) we met some of the entrants who had begun their day at Postbridge—clad in wellies and trainers (on their feet!) and in an assortment of plastic macs, coats, headwear and nether-garments. From this tor, we carried on along the path until near Winter Tor. This pile is on the left of the track only thirty metres from it and nearly opposite the southernmost tor of the Belstone range to the right, Higher Tor. We veered left to pass west of Winter Tor and headed towards Cullever Steps where a track fords the Okement. This is another popular place for visitors because cars can be driven to the river's edge (606921).

The most direct way towards the next checkpoint is to keep on the right bank of the Okement and to the east of Scarey Tor, the obvious pile ahead of you. The track leading off to the right in a north-easterly direction goes to Belstone and is also used by the army when the red warning flag is shown on Watchet Hill. We continued across some short turf, marshy in places, to Chapel Ford (608934). Here yet another track approaches from the hill toward the river. When I last saw the ford, the depth of water would have flooded the distributor of a Land Rover. The modern footbridge is now crossed and another well-defined path is followed through Halstock Wood for the next mile (1.5 km) as far as Fatherford Viaduct (603947). Underneath the arches, the marshals dream their dreams away, whilst above, the railway is used by trucks going to and from Meldon Quarry. The Carboniferous Culm Measures in the quarry face are used as ballast in supporting railway sleepers. The pity of this line is that the permanent way would have been ideal for a one-way traffic-flow. A better-signed Holiday Route in addition would have made all arguments concerning an Oke-hampton by-pass un-necessary.

Checking in for the last time, we turned left through a gate and on the north bank of the Okement made our way under Ball Hill. This well-used path,

The path beneath Ball Hill

so close to the destination, must be a godsend to OATS walkers, being easy to follow and not too undulating at the end of a long day's walking. The path passes Okehampton School and the entrance to Simmond's Park on the left.

Now, on the pavements of Okehampton, the feet may ache but the thoughts of completing the course, or of a free cup of something, and that of shaking hands with the town's mayor, help to maintain a steady pace. Or could it be that you are walking downhill? Entering Tors Road and passing the local "nick" we faced the crowd of well-wishers and made for Charter Hall where, at last, we could relax, sit down in comfort and chat with the earlier finishers. The walk described was undertaken the year after the first completion of the OATS walk, the details of which appear overleaf.

ITINERARY

Checkpoints	Approx Time	Accumulative Distance		Grid Refs
		km	(miles)	
New Waste	8.00			625611
(Cross R. Erme)	9.00	5.25	(3.25)	636660
Fish Lake	9.20	8.0	(5.0)	647682
Ter Hill-cross	9.50	10.5	(6.5)	642707
Hexworthy	10.30	13.5	(8.5)	655726
Postbridge	11.50	20.75	(13.0)	646788
(Grey Wethers)	1.00	26.0	(16.25)	639831
Quintin's Man	1.35	28.0	(17.5)	622838
Site of O.P.16	2.35	32.0	(20.0)	613874
Cullever Steps	3.30	37.0	(23.0)	606922
Fatherford Viaduct	4.30	40.0	(25.0)	603947
Charter Hall	5.00	42.0	(26.25)	587553

N.B. Time taken out for stops: 1 hour 40 mins

5

The Perambulation

Historical Background

This is probably the oldest and certainly the longest "set" walk on Dartmoor, unless you include the rare activity established by the Long-Distance Walkers' Association of the "100", an annual hundred-mile walk which takes place in various parts of the country (details later). The idea to perambulate came from King Henry III, no less, who said, in so many words, to his knights, 'Look here, chaps, I've got this piece of property in Devon, but I want to know how big it is. I'm not going wenching or hunting if the locals are going to shout out, "Hey you, get off my land! Can't you read?". So be good fellows and trot off and make a definite boundary line between my forest and the commoners' land.'

Twelve knights then set off and began to ride around the forest bounds, starting from Cosdon (Cawsand on many maps, unfortunately) Beacon. This was as good a place as any, because travellers from the east would see the huge rounded bulk of this hill from some way off. "That must be the moor", they would say, and zoom up to it to have a good view of the countryside. Given good weather, Exmoor, The Blackdown Hills, much of North Dartmoor, High Willhays, Yes Tor and the north of Cornwall are visible. Hence, the establishing of a beacon on the summit. The Silver Jubilee celebrations in 1977 were crowned in more ways than one by the lighting of a fire on the hill top when the counterpart on Dunkery Beacon, Exmoor, was seen to be lit up. The glow in the sky was visible from Ugborough Beacon, overlooking Bittaford, 21 miles away to the south.

There are no actual checkpoints

37

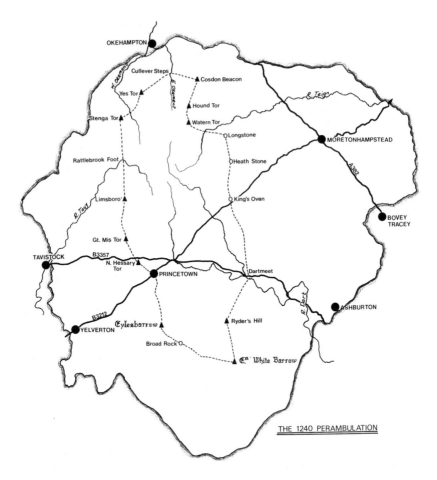

OKEHAMPTON

Cullever Steps
Cosdon Beacon
Yes Tor ▲
Hound Tor ▲
Stenga Tor ▲
Watern Tor ▲
○Longstone
MORETONHAMPSTEAD
Rattlebrook Foot
○Heath Stone
Limsboro' ▲
○King's Oven
BOVEY
TRACEY
Gt. Mis Tor ▲
B3357
N. Hessary ▲
Tor
PRINCETOWN
Dartmeet
TAVISTOCK
B3212
Eylesbarrow ▲
Ryder's Hill ▲
YELVERTON
Broad Rock ○
ASHBURTON
Eⁿ White Barrow ▲

THE 1240 PERAMBULATION

on this walk; no-one is waiting to give you encouragement, a cup of coffee or a tent. There is, however, a list of points which you should visit, complete with 1240 spellings and Grid references, and a space to enter the times of arrival at each site. It is possible, just, to complete the trek in one day—it's pushing it and not advisable if you don't know the moor very well. You can read the GRs and estimate the time it will take, but Dartmoor terrain is not shown on any maps that I've come across. We completed the walk in two days fairly comfortably with a break in between to watch the 1983 Grand National. There are ways of proving your journey and the organiser, Ian Kirkpatrick, will probably suggest one or two. The following is

the account I wrote immediately after receiving my badge and certificate. My companion was Dennis Johnston, an older, but wiser, friend.

It isn't often that I get really drenched—I mean, like everyone else, I take my annual bath and enjoy the experience and, preferring to keep my feet firmly on the ground, I do less swimming than in the past. So, on reflection, being saturated not once but twice in succession is a novel event; the circumstances were quite different.

Dennis and I had hoped to perambulate the 1240 Forest Bounds of Dartmoor back in September. Then, the early fog persisted all morning and determined the abandonment of the venture after four hours. The actual route is fixed in that thirty three locations should be visited and the time noted at each. The distance works out at nearly sixty miles, or 95 km, and our intention was to walk the slightly greater part on the Friday—on the north Moor—then "do" the rest of the tour on the Sunday.

Rain clouds threatened the initial stages but the showers that seemed to be developing over Bodmin Moor didn't materialise; in fact, the sun came out and stayed with us for much of the day. Leaving Rundlestone (574750) just outside Princetown at nine o'clock, we made our way northwards to Great Mis Tor (563769), White Barrow (568798) and Lynch Tor (566805) where we had decided to have our first short stop. The intention of starting at an "easy" pace to last the day was ignored as we covered the six kilometres to Lynch in an hour. You'll soon realise that I prefer the modern measurements when working from a map—much easier than translating yards into miles or chains into inches! Bearing almost due north we aimed for Outer Redlake to turn down the Tavy to Rattlebrook Foot (561837). The terrain, from being a fairly well-worn path from Lynch Tor, became marshy and heather-covered, especially on the level parts. (Yes, there are "level" parts on Dartmoor, but they have not yet been vetted by the MCC.) Following up the Rattlebrook on the west bank (less marsh than on the east), we

39

The bleak ruins of Bleak House on a cold and bleak Dartmoor day

realised that due to our storming start, we were already nearly half-an-hour ahead of schedule, and with the weather brightening considerably, we made our way to Bleak House (559865) reaching it in need of a drink. This ruin was the home of peat-cutters during the last two centuries; now it's a target both for the army, when they fire live ammunition, and for the Ten Tors trainees who use it as a "convenient" spot for dining and for "watering their horses". Hence the hideous assortment of polybags, cans, Andrex and Alcan.

All this time, we had been travelling in a northerly direction, and you can't perambulate anything without turning corners. Rattlebrook Head was to be our first deviation and we then set out towards Stenga Tor (568880). Below this outcrop is the West Okement River, and on a previous visit I found difficulty in crossing it. After much searching up and down for a *safe* place to cross without injury I found a likely spot. I thought that three strides from bank to boulders to bank would see me across. Dennis obviously thought otherwise and kindly held back to let me go first. My first step was fairly safe but I must have been standing on the string of my gaiter as I tried to take another small step for mankind. I'm not saying the water was deep, but my right arm and leg didn't touch the bottom (of the river)—my left-sided limbs were draped around the rock in what must have seemed to Dennis to be a rather erotic position. A minute later, he waded through!

The toughest climb of the day up to High Willhays and Yes Tor (581902) came immediately. The "roof of Devon" in all its glory was the high-spot of the day. A longer stop in the army shed at Fordsland Ledge was taken to

dry off. What with crossing rivers and climbing precipitous slopes, our speed had decreased to below 3 kph but we had made allowances—or rather Dennis had, as he explained Naysmith's law. We were able to cross the Black-aven Brook and the East Okement River (606921) by footbridge and then there followed another steep climb over the Belstone Ridge. By now, we were half-way round the first day's route and our way led over the Taw River ford, which, by this time, held no trepidations as we splashed through. Another stiff climb to Cosdon Beacon (635915) was made at a steadily decreasing pace, but there was pleasure once more as we reached the summit—not just admiring the panoramic views over North and East Devon, but just to give our limbs a rest. Thankfully, it was nearly all downhill from here and still within thirty minutes of our plan, the aches were temporarily forgotten. Here, also we turned south and faced our first day's destination 8 miles—sorry, thirteen kilometres—away.

The south face of Cosdon is nothing to write home about, so I won't. We arrived at Hound Tor (629890) to have a quick drink—I mention this tor for two reasons. This outcrop was formerly known as "Parva Hunde torre" or the "little tor on the hundred", and is *not* the tourist attraction where the BBC recently serialised "the Hound of the Baskervilles". *That* Hound Tor is a magnificent group of rocks. The other reason is that, as proof of us visiting the points stated, we had stamped our papers with some "letterbox" prints. At Hound Tor this is easy to locate, but at this time of year (April) many are removed before the souvenir-hunters, going under the name of Ten Tor expeditions, get their hands on them.

41

The next part of the walk was relatively uneventful; passing Wild Tor Well, crossing the Walla Brook, resting at Watern Tor (629869), fording the Teign at Hewlake foot and slogging eastwards to the Longstone (660857). But the knights on horseback who perambulated in the 13th century didn't have a reservoir to cross. The ancient forest and modern parish boundaries both go across Fernworthy Reservoir.

Having had one soaking already, we crossed the outflowing stream by footbridge and arrived at the Heath Stone (671837). Here, one of the men who was working on the dam before the war had given vent to his grateful feelings and had carved in granite a text from St Matthew's Gospel, much to the annoyance of the authorities.

Heading up and across Chagford Common, and passing near the cairns on Hurston Ridge, we approached King's Oven and the Warren House Inn (673812). This pub was our final port of call for the day and we arrived warm and thirsty, to be picked up and driven home. End of part one, and what an enjoyable experience—a good long walk, excellent weather throughout, glorious views, good company and a sense of achievement.

That was the chalk; the cheese came on the Sunday. Well, the forecast was reasonable but the weather wasn't. We began, in light showers and a moderate breeze in our faces, from the Warren House and followed the right bank of the Wallabrook, crossing to the left bank at Runnage. As on Friday, we started the day on easy terrain and made very good time—most of the route was on footpaths as the boundary followed the river, threading its way through enclosures, private land or marsh. After passing around Rogue's Roost and through Sherrill, we

came to Dartmeet (672731) where we made our first break. While we were eating the sun broke through, but the clouds to the south over Holne Ridge were low and threatening.

Deciding not to swim across the Dart at Week Ford (663724), where the stepping-stones were apparently under the flood-waters of the previous day's rain, we walked through Hexworthy and down to Soldier's Bridge to follow

the O Brook upstream. Then, the worst of the perambulation fell upon us; talk about "Apres moi le deluge", it tipped down and trudging up to Ryders Hill (660691) with the wind, hail and rain in our faces I felt more and more dispirited. I tentatively suggested abandoning our venture, but with most of the difficult climbing over and done with, we could complete the course by keeping to valleys and fairly well-sheltered passes. Over a coffee-break at Huntingdon Warren on the Western Wallabrook (665670), we finally decided to carry on. The rain was less heavy but the clouds were lower.

We crossed the Avon and, going west, met the former rail-track which led from the southern borders of the moor to the china-clay workings at isolated Redlake. We were just within our planned schedule and, stopping at Erme Head (622669) in the shelter of the

tinners' heaps for another snack, we thought that our troubles were behind us. We are both familiar with this area, but we were thwarted by the fog. Coming out of the clouds, we met a group of schoolboys approaching from the north and aiming for Venford Reservoir, to the north-east. We were at Broad Rock, between high ground to north and south, the Erme valley on the east and the Plym to the west. Here is

West solle Forest 1240 Perambulation

where we could have made good use of our compasses but we had progressed a further five minutes before we realised that a bearing on to Eylesbarrow, our next port of call, would have seen us right. Instead, we made the mistake of thinking that if we walked due west we would meet the Plym and would follow it up river to Plym Ford and we could then walk up to Eylesbarrow.

So we walked on, crossed two or three small streams, found a leat, followed it and bore north, passed a cairn—and stopped. The fog was just as thick, less than twenty paces visibility and, deciding that we were "hopelessly confused", as Dennis put it, we headed due north. I said that we *had* to meet the mine track even if we had already crossed the Plym without realising it. We'd only progressed on our new bearing for a minute when dark, tree-shaped objects loomed ahead. They were trees surrounding a building, the first we'd seen since Hexworthy. A little notice on the door, in faded felt-tip ink read, "Ditsworthy Adventure Centre". I recognised it then, from our holiday haunt at nearby Sheepstor, but it meant that we should have to travel three miles (5 km) extra, even if we went on the most direct route from here back to Princetown and the Rundlestone. This was, thankfully, by way of the mine track which we followed for three-quarters of an hour. We stopped for a welcome rest under cover in Nun's Cross Farm (606699). This nineteenth century building is being renovated to accommodate services and youth groups on expedition training. Reaching the metalled road (Castle Lane) near Peat Cot, it meant that the remaining seven kilometres were to be on asphalt. In the end, we arrived where we had started two-and-a-half days ago, only a few minutes later than our unofficial plan.

Still, although soaked to the skin once again, it was an unforgettable experience—and there's a smart badge to go with the certificate. It would be nice to do the second part (properly) in fine weather, but, for that moment, the sense of achievement took pride of place.

ITINERARY

Official Route	Approx Time	Accumulative* Distance km	(miles)	Grid Refs
Rundlestone	9.00			574750
Great Mis Tor	9.20			563769
White Barrow	9.50			568798
Limsboro' Cairn	10.05	6.0	(3.75)	566805
Rattlebrook Foot	10.50	9.25	(5.75)	561837
Rattlebrook Head	11.40	12.25	(7.75)	(Bleak House)
Stenga Tor	12.05	14.25	(9.0)	568880
Sandy Ford	12.30			
	12.45	16.25	(10.0)	(Fordsland)
Yes Tor	1.35	18.0	(11.25)	581902
Cullever Steps	2.25	20.5	(13.0)	606921
Cosdon (Cawsand) Beacon	3.30	23.5	(14.75)	636915
Hound Tor	3.50	26.25	(16.5)	629890
Watern Tor	4.25			629869
Hewlake Foot	4.40	30.25	(19.0)	640860
Long Stone	5.10			660857
Heath Stone	6.10	35.25	(22.0)	671837
Chagford Common	6.45			671830
King's Oven	7.00: 9.00	39.0	(24.5)	(Warren House)
Wallabrook Head				676810
Wallabrook Foot	10.00	44.0	(27.5)	(Cator Gate)
Dartmeet	10.50	48.0	(30.0)	672731
Week Ford	11.20			(Hexworthy)
Drylake Foot	11.55	52.5	(33.0)	661710
B.S. on Sandyway	12.25			659696
Ryders Hill	12.35			660691
W. Wallabrook Head	12.45	55.25	(34.5)	665685
W. Wallabrook Foot	1.20			665662
Redlake Foot	2.35	60.25	(37.75)	636661
Erme Head Ford	2.55	62.0	(38.75)	622669
Eylesbarrow Cairn	4.00	66.0	(41.25)	(Ditsworthy AC)
Nun's Cross	4.45	70.0	(43.75)	605699
Princetown	5.50	77.25	(48.5)	(Princetown)
Rundlestone	6.15	79.75	(50.0)	574750

Time taken out for stops: 1st Day—1hour 35 mins; 2nd Day—45 mins
*Distance measured on map, not on the ground

6

Tom Cobley's Walk

Pseudo-Historical Background

This is a semi-official event—not organised by a committee for the participation of hundreds, but a regular walk undertaken occasionally by a few groups, some of which are obsessed with arriving at Widecombe at opening time.

The folk song "Widecombe Fair", heard and written down by Rev. Sabine Baring-Gould, tells of a group of men who decided to visit the village (to let their hair down, we assume) and participate in the fun. The verses infer that all the named personnel lived in one area some distance from Widecombe, but the singer is included among the would-be travellers as an extra. He names Bill Brewer, Jan Stewer, Peter Gurney, Peter Davy, Daniel Whiddon, Harry Hawke and Tom Cobley and sings that he wants to go with them. Tom Pearse owns the nag. From the size of Spreyton where they traditionally lived, half the men of the village were in other quarters on that day—it must have been quiet on the Spreyton green. So, if they all went on horseback, (and no wonder the old grey mare passed on!) which way did they go? At the instigation of Chips Barber, and the determination of Dennis Johnston who scouted the likely route, a twenty-mile walk was established. No doubt you will be amazed that a horse carrying six or seven men at a time could cope with the countryside between Spreyton and Widecombe.

A group of six of us congregated outside the Tom Cobley Inn (698967) one Sunday morning and proceeded west for about 300 paces before turning left down a wide signposted bridlepath. In the same distance we forked left, crossed two minute tributaries of the River Yeo, and turned left in the middle of Nethercott Farm to follow the path southwards. A couple of right-angled turns brought us to a minor, but important, road into which we turned left and strode along for half a mile before turning right. (Brandis Cross 688939). Another half mile along this lane took us to a narrow track to the left near the top of a gentle rise. Ahead lay Dartmoor with Cosdon Hill most prominent. A right turn found us at another lane

46

at which we turned left and walked downhill looking out carefully for the "Footpath" sign pointing right. We found it in a hedge but assumed—correctly as it happened—that the right of way, according to our maps, lay in that direction. The path narrowed, became muddier and overgrown with undergrowth, until we emerged between two hedges and found ourselves at Addiscott. We turned left to face a steep uphill climb towards the A30 but at Firestone Cross (668930) we didn't feel too "tyred".

Ahead lay Dartmoor and open air. I prefer to walk on open land and to lessen the distance on lanes and between enclosures, but we had some way to go before that situation could arise. Crossing the main road and taking a right fork at the next junction, we found ourselves speeding our paces as the valley of the Blackaton Brook lay in front. At the next junction, we turned left and again noted a footpath sign to the right pointing along a hedge. This we followed, passed through the hedge to follow its other side, and bore slightly left across the field to the brook. A newish footbridge now spans the water and the path is quite distinct as it conducted us to a gate and a farm track. On meeting yet

47

another lane, we turned left again and walked into Throwleigh. Keeping right, close to the wall of the churchyard, we found ourselves going uphill before meeting a wooden signpost denoting "Mariner's Way". (See that particular walk for details.) We turned left here into what locals call "Deave Lane" (667907). It certainly is devious; a false sense of security is felt along the initial stages ("This is easy", "Boring", "Where's the view?") but we encountered several veritable pits of very wet ground. Not the healthy black peat of the open moor, but a mini-morass of soil, humus from the hedgerow and other deposits. Eventually we emerged near Wonson, looking back to remark bitterly on a sign reading, "No entry for wide vehicles".

Bearing left onto the next lane and passing a coach-hire firm (what, out here, miles from civilisation?) and the Chapel of Providence on the left, we bore right onto another track and steeply descended into Coombe, meeting another road. We turned left, crossed Moortown Brook and immediately turned right to Gidleigh Mill. Another climb confronted us—did the grey mare do *all* this?—and we emerged much warmer at a grey telephone box at Gidleigh (672884). Ahead was the spired church but not being inspired to

Throwleigh Church.

visit it we turned left onto—yes, another road, turning right at another junction to look for another footpath sign. We had only had a five-minute pause up to now and our thirsts needed some quenching. "We'll get onto the moor first," someone muttered. Turning left we found ourselves in cooling conifers and, seeing that we could follow the ubiquitous orange blobs, did so bearing gradually to the right and dropping steeply down to the North Teign valley. Before the footbridge was erected, the crossing was necessarily made over "Glassy Steps" (672875), stepping stones not characterised by their opaque qualities but more, I should imagine, by their inability to support a size 8 boot. A right-angled crossing of a youthful river usually means steep down/steep up and this part of the journey was no exception. Thankfully, most of the route to date was easy to follow and all exertion was of the physical type. Emerging onto yet another road, we encountered another "Mariner's Way" legend on a signpost and followed the point to the moor walking, in effect, straight on.

In two hundred yards we turned right into Teigncombe Lane where we encountered the roughest terrain to date with large boulders, brambles and a steep climb up to the moor. We followed the track and kept the wall on our left hand and, turning south, passed the little forest on the lefthand corner. If you are in no particular hurry go on up to the tor, Kestor Rock (666863), and walk from tor to tor in a south east direction. Otherwise, walk SSE from the corner toward the next pile, Middle Tor, continuing in the same direction past Frenchbeer Rock (672854) to cross the lane and steeply drop down to the South Teign. We crossed by a well-worn log placed conveniently over the water but, our day being one of several successive dry ones, the river could have been negotiated by stepping stones. We followed the wall on our left, up the other bank as it bends to the east, emerging through a gate onto a track which meets the road from Chagford to Fernworthy Reservoir, near Yardworthy (679848). We turned right and followed the road for a few hundred yards but kept the wall close to our left until it angled away to the east. The next part of the walk was a slog with few items of interest to note. We walked south for half-a-mile, then bore slightly to the right so that we went along the ridge between the Metherall Brook on our right and the North Walla Brook on our left. We walked south again but kept above the steeper bank of the North Walla until we met some gullies as the ground levels out to the east of Water Hill. From many angles on the hill the chimneys of Warren House were visible. King's Oven, the site of hectic mining activity in Tudor times, is marked by two very deep and wide grassy gullies which face the road. The optional choice of inn or gully depends on the time you arrive or the amount of thirst. We were too late!

We looked for the telephone posts which stride out down the moor away from the road. Nearby is a gravel track with a low bar across. We followed this until, where it bears left, a steep rough path led ahead and down towards a wide grassy valley bottom with a tun-

The famous Warren House Inn

nelled stream, ruins of tinners' and miners' huts. We followed the path which touches the east wall and then bore left toward the telegraph poles. From here, the route was well-worn—soon the buildings of Headland Warren Farm (693812) were in sight as well as a road which runs along the slope of the opposite bank. In less than a quarter-of-a-mile the Iron Age village of Grimspound was reached (701808). We walked through the wall, not over it, and out of the pound to the south to make our last ascent, up to Hameldown Tor. From here for the next two miles was easy; a well-worn earth track follows the ridge to the south passing guide-stones and barrows and a view on either side added interest. We followed the path downhill to a track which joins from the left and a wall which approaches behind it. Where this track divides, we walked steeply down and kept the angles of the wall as our guide. We made for the gate at the top of the track between two walls and followed it downhill for a quarter of a mile, turning right at the bottom to triumphantly enter the centre of Widecombe village.

No, Tom Pearse and his fellow-travellers did *not* come this way. They would surely have kept to the lower parts of the moor, probably following the Mariners' Way (q.v.) all the way from Frenchbeer and Yardworthy Moorgate. But don't tell the others—they wanted an "open moorland" walk and opted for this diversion purely for devilment.

ITINERARY

	Approx Time	Accumulative Distance km	(miles)	Grid Refs
Spreyton	10.15			698967
Firestone Cross	11.25	6.75	(4.25)	668930
Gidleigh		12.25	(7.75)	672884
Kestor	1.00			666863
Yardworthy	2.00	17.25	(11.00)	679848
Warren House	2.45	21.75	(13.75)	673809
Grimspound	3.25	24.75	(15.50)	700809
Widecombe	4.30	30.00	(18.75)	718767

Time for stops: 45 mins.

7

Animal Crackers—North

Background Information

It is surprising how, over the years on the moor, local accents and descriptive names have evolved into so many names of animals. A walk of 13 miles will take you to a rabbit (or a deer), a French cat (un chat) and three other members of the cat family, and a connection with volpine and canine breeds as well as a herd of elephants. No need for an admission price to any wildlife park or zoo; the names do not by any means indicate the abundance of that animal in the vicinity. At least, the hope is that some of the furry creatures suggested are not loose on the hills. Hare Tor, as an example of derivative names, is said to be a corruption of "Higher Tor", noting a comparison with the neighbouring Sharp, Ger and Nat Tors. William Crossing believes that Dunna Goat, overlooking Bleak House, is derived from "dun" (hill) and "coed" (wood). However, the OS names are also verbal evolutions and so with some licence let's go big-game hunting.

Start at the Dartmoor Inn (523853) on the main road between Okehampton and Tavistock and take the track leading to the moor, a little to the north of the inn (signposted). Passing between shrubs and under branches, arrive at a gate through which cars *do* pass to park on High Down itself—a practice to which, at the time of writing, the National Park Committee appears to turn a blind eye. Walk off the tracks and on the grass, going east until, noticing Widgery Cross on Brat Tor ahead of you, you drop down fairly steeply into the valley of the River Lyd. Walk downstream, passing a cliff, on your right, and Hunter's Plaque (more of which is said under the Memorial Walk). Cross the river here and on the opposite cliff, which is more gravelly than the west bank, pick up the grassy path, walking south. The path veers gradually away from the Lyd as the valley of the Doe Tor Brook is approached, and drops down to cross that stream by a concrete bridge. On gaining the other side, walk upstream, avoiding wherever possible climbing walls of the private enclosures which once formed the land under the ownership of Doe Tor Farm. The piles of granite ahead, and a little to the right as you walk, is that tor (542848).

Black Rock on the River Lyd

After the Doe comes the Hare: for Hare Tor (551842) walk south-east for three-quarters of a mile. Any stone pillars, about 3 feet high, that you pass will indicate the bounds of the Willsworthy Rifle Range before the red-and-white poles were erected. The stones are numbered after "WD" on one side and there are over 40 of them. Walking from Hare Tor for nearly one mile at 25° you will arrive at Chat Tor. En route, after about 500 yards, is a well-preserved cairn (552845). Chat Tor (556853) is a single mass of granite forming an almost regular cone, the apex of which conceals a letterbox (Dartmoor type) with a stamp of annually-changing design. It is usually the head of a cat (of course), sometimes accompanied by "Happy Christmas" at that season.

Two goats are visible from here. They overlook the valley of the Rattlebrook—on your right—and are approached on a bearing of 7° from Chat. You pass a range noticeboard warning of the dangers of picking up any metal objects found on the moor (such as range noticeboards?). Cross a sunken track—a path formed by peat-

53

wagons from Amicombe Hill and mine-workers from Rattlebrook tin mine—just half-a-mile downstream from Bleak House. Continue up the hill to the tors.

Between Lower and Higher Dunnagoat (558865) is a boundary stone denoting the limits of Lydford parish, to the south and east, and Sowton parish. Bleak House, in the valley, will be visited during another excursion. You will not have failed to notice some very impressive piles of rock in the distance to the north on the walk from Hare Tor to Chat Tor to Dunnagoat. And no doubt, you will have thought, "Wouldn't it be nice to go and explore those rocks; what

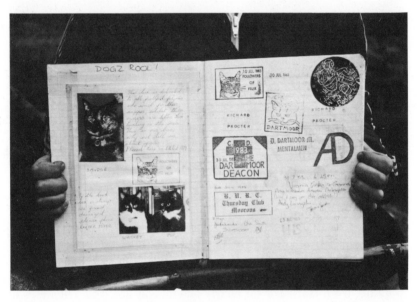

sort of view would I get from there?" Off you go then, you don't need instructions, but a straight line will take you across some peat ties. If you didn't see any rocks, go up the slope from Dunnagoat to the north-west. Great Links (or Lynx, if you want the spelling of the animal corrected) is at 551867.

From here, the next animal to see is a smaller version of this one, Kitty Tor, visible from Great Links on 65° and just over a mile distant. On the way, you will again enter the military range, crossing the line of red-and-white poles. For a drier route to the tor, walk north-east for a few hundred paces, to meet the track of the Rattlebrook Peat railway, and follow it downhill (east) to cross the brook by bridge and pass between ruins of the works. The area has seen great activity in the past, but always the conditions above and below the ground have prevailed and most schemes to turn the peat into a profitable commodity have failed. The last effort was between 1952 and 1956. Making your way up to Kitty Tor (567875), with its army hut and a flagpole further to the south of it, you would pass many turf-ties and peat hags which scar the hillside. These would make the going more difficult if you were approaching from Bleak House. From Kitty Tor there are some fine views across the West Okement valley, north-east towards High Willhays and Yes Tor, and in the opposite direction to the tors you have just visited. They make a contrast with the bleak and desolate scene to the south and north-west which may have caused so many enterprises to fail. It could easily occur to the walker that whichever way you proceed from here will involve some tough terrain. But the flagpole, like that

The Rattlebrook near Bleak House

at Hare Tor, is frequently used, and the army, being human, use the easiest form of transport to arrive at the poles and raise warning flags when firing takes place. Four-wheel drive vehicles rumble across the moors at first light and consequently a track of some sort is eroded. That which approaches Kitty Tor is found to the north-west and it will act as a guide to the next point. Before you set out, notice a small tor, almost due west, three-quarters of a mile away. The track will eventually arrive at the tor, although not in a direct line. The track was also used in the nineteenth century by peat-cutters. It goes north-west to Gren Tor, (so do you), passing over Woodcock Hill. In under half-a-mile, the track becomes slightly sunken. Here, veer off to the right (north) into the upper valley of the River Lyd, where it oozes through a boggy area called Tiger's

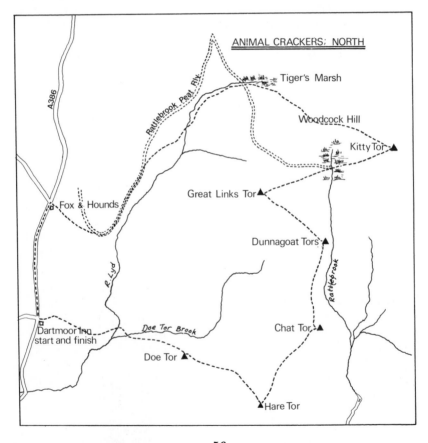

Marsh. It is not a name which appears on OS maps, but Crossing mentions it in his "Guide to Dartmoor". The Marsh is at 554882.

Follow the stream down for two miles. First, you meet and cross the Rattlebrook Peat Railway near Gren Tor and, as the valley widens, several remains of tin-miners' activities are passed, including "The Hut", a cache for their tools. It is simply an arrangement of rocks to form a sunken cave and is about 100 yards from the river on the east bank (543877). Later, the valley narrows as the Lyd runs between Great Nodden to the west and the hill topped by Great Links Tor to the east. Just over half-a-mile past Great Nodden a track crosses the river at a ford. Follow this to the south-west and, as it turns to the west, approach the peat railway track again and pass a small reservoir. The track is now stony and well-used by locals and tourists alike. It goes through a gate and between a hedge, on your right, and open farmland on the left, to approach the main road (A386) at the "Fox and Hounds" (cheat!). If you have timed your walk to arrive when the pub is open, the chances are that on your last mile south, down the road to the Dartmoor Inn, you will have added to the list of animals considerably, being accompanied by pink elephants. However don't trust your luck; the road is fast, busy, and motorists don't always look out for animal collectors when they're about their business.

ROUTE

	Accumulative Distance		Grid Refs
	km	(miles)	
Dartmoor Inn			523853
Doe Tor	3.0	(2.0)	542848
Hare Tor	4.5	(3.0)	551842
Chat Tor	5.75	(3.5)	556853
Dunnagoat Tors	7.0	(4.5)	558865
Great "Lynx" Tor	7.75	(5.0)	551867
Kitty Tor	10.0	(6.25)	567875
Woodcock Hill	11.25	(7.0)	sq55-87
Tiger's Marsh	12.25	(7.75)	554882
Fox and Hounds	16.5	(10.0)	525867
Dartmoor Inn	18.0	(11.0)	523853

8

Animal Crackers—South

Background Information

Continuing the theme of visiting locations named (seemingly) after animals, an alternative trek can be visualised on the southern moor, although even more licence must be granted to include insects and birds. Four of our feathered friends are featured forthwith along with four-footed creatures. This is another circular walk—lasting all day if you stroll—and, unlike the previous amble, takes in some of the grander parts of the uplands and approaches the wilder areas of the "Southern Morass", as some guide-books call it. (The morass really means the area with little or no rocky outcrops; rather, flatter terrain with fewer features to identify.) In other words, it is a get-away-from-everyone tour.

An ideal point at which to start is at Burcombe Gate (577673) which is approached best from Burrator Reservoir, through Sheepstor village, between high walls as the road climbs and, as it emerges at a sharp right-hand corner, turn left passing the "No Through Road" sign. Follow the lane for about half-a-mile to where there is a parking place for a few cars, (or two coaches!). The tor crowning the scene to the south is Gutter Tor. Alighting from your vehicle, follow the stony track which passes it by on the east (left), just across the river from a clump of pine trees surrounding a hut, which is the Ditsworthy Adventure Centre (see Perambulation Walk). Walk along the track facing more or less south, cross over Gutter Tor Mire and enter the Plym Valley. A mile (1.5 km) from the lane, the track veers left, meeting a wall running up from the valley bottom. Keep right of the wall and follow a slightly less obvious path to cross the river at a ford, and cross the Lee Moor Leat by a recently-restored bridge. Your first "bird" has been visible for nearly all the walk, by the way. It can be caught ahead of you, and just to your left, at the top of the hill. Hen Tor (594653) can be approached from the leat by a variety of paths; it doesn't need precise instructions. Words of warning, though: beware of tall fern in summer. A sign of once-cultivated land, it is difficult to follow a given path through the bracken. Care is also advised, as you approach the tor, of a larger area of clitter—a twisted ankle is no fun at the best of times, especially when you have appointments to keep with some birds.

From Hen Tor, few directions are needed to arrive at the next "animal"; you have an alternative to a compass bearing of 35°, for which you could be thankful, if you want a bee-line, Roman Road type of route. Instead, walk due north for half-a-mile to meet the Shavercombe valley which you follow downstream to meet a path leading up the south-east bank of the Plym. Follow it upstream for one mile, to the next tributary entering the Plym from the south-east, (the Langcombe Brook) noticing on the opposite bank, a large cairn (Giant's Basin), some smaller ones further up the hill, and three menhirs—the tallest of which is just over 14 feet (4 metres), the biggest on Dartmoor. All three terminate stone rows which each lead to the smaller cairns. These constitute the most impressive paleolithic group of the moor, if not in Britain. Termed a "sanctuary", it overshadows other such sites at Shovel Down and Longash Hill, near Merrivale.

Cross the Langcombe near Plym Steps, where monks and other travellers going west from Buckfast Abbey were said to have crossed their penultimate water course. The group of tors standing sentinel over the parent river on the right bank may be approached up the north bank, or appreciated from the south of the Plym. They are the Hart Tors, or, in the vernacular, Harter Tors (603675). They bear no resemblance to deer but then, neither does the next port of call. As you follow the river, another small group of mini-tors—miniators?—appear on the slope ahead (608676). These rocks form Calveslake Tor and one assumes that the "lake", or river, nearby (to the north) is frequently occupied by young cattle. This might be the only animal name on the moor which has the depicted creature in view as, on many occasions that I have visited this site, I have been in the presence of young (and old) bovine residents. Walking up the hill ENE—approximately 70°—you approach and reach Great Gnats Head (617679) in three-quarters of a mile (1 km). I suppose you may be accompanied by gnats on a hot day, but it depends on the state of the vegetation in the area and flies are certainly abundant around ancient cowpats in the vicinity. Continuing due east, the ground slopes gently away in front of you and you (re-) discover Ducks' Pool (628678). Refer to walk No. 8B when the approach is from another direction. The "pool" is described on those pages.

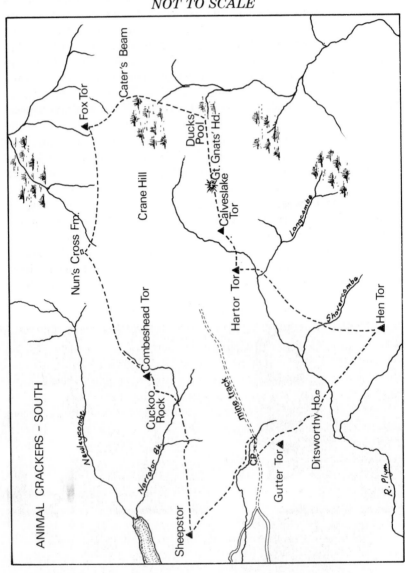

At this point, you can choose either to make a right-angled turn and begin to make tracks for base, or you may visit Fish Lake as another creature included in the "animal" theme but, should you choose to do the latter, be warned that the going in both Summer and Winter is tough and more tiring than the terrain up to this point. In winter the ground is squelchy and in parts, marshy; in warmer weather the summer growth of vegetation impedes your walking, and a regular pace is difficult to maintain. For Fish Lake, from Ducks' Pool, walk due east for a mile, when a shallow depression is apparent just to your left running east as well. This is the valley of the stream just named and in another half-mile the renowned tinners' hut is reached (647681). A notice inside the roofless ruin states that the letterbox is not in the hut as in former times, so don't "rooflessly" pull the place to pieces. From here, a walk due north-west, of two miles, over the desolate waste of Naker's Hill and across the valley of the Upper Swincombe valley, will see you at Fox Tor.

The more direct route from Ducks' Pool goes almost due north, but the ground is inclined to be soggy, except after long dry spells. I have twice been able to follow Blacklane Brook, on the west bank, to

Ducks' Pool Letterbox lunatics

Caters Beam but on other occasions I had to cross the brook, after walking north-east from Ducks' Pool for about five hundred yards, and take a more meandering track northwards. Eventually, on the skyline, an upright wooden pole becomes visible and whether on the left or right bank, make for it as best as you can. It proves to be a railway sleeper—or, as it's inscribed "Cater's Beam", it should be a buffet car. But "beam" on the moor is the remains of tinners' working, and you can't cater for inaccuracies in the wilds of the moor. The pole, in fact, stands at the northernmost point of an old peat-workers' path leading from the Erme, two miles away. (The 1984 Dartmoor Leisure Map, 1:25000, is more accurate than previous editions in its siting of the marker-pole.) From here, continue slightly west of north down a gully towards the pile of rocks on the near horizon, but avoid a deep gully traversing your route. The bottom is always marshy so a few paces to the left on the top of the bank, before bee-lining for the tor, is the best way. Fox Tor (626699) overlooks Childe's Tomb to the north (see the North-South Walk), and Foxtor Mires.

Make your way to Nun's Cross Farm, walking on the north slope of Crane Hill (another "animal" but another area of clinging vegetation), keeping the enclosure wall well away on your right. Cross three gullies, which dip to the north, before climbing up to the Devonport Leat and the not-so imposing Nun's Cross Farm. Beyond the building, to the west Siward's Cross will give you a guide to the next objective.

From the cross, walk south-west for about a mile and a half (2 km), most of which is slightly downhill, with the Dean Combe on your right, to another tor, Combeshead, which has two or three cave-like crevices facing you as you approach. Three hundred yards due west, a triangular rock rises from the bracken about 20 feet high with an additional rock on the apex, appearing to be an after-thought by its creator, but not quite fitting the smooth outline of its supporter. Cuckoo Rock (585687) is the site of another original letterbox, but you'd get the bird if you tried to climb up to its original position. The last port of call is probably the most impressive tor in this part of the moor, certainly on this particular jaunt.

From Cuckoo Rock walk downhill (south) and, following a path through the undergrowth, pass through the ruins of Deancombe Farm, find the stream and a small wooden hut, near which is a crossing place consisting of stepping stones. Take the path leading south and in 200 yards cross the Deancombe Brook, a tributary of the Narrator Brook. Climb steeply, veering right as you do so, until, where the ground becomes less steep, walking westwards you approach a right-angled wall. Don't climb over but walk alongside it reaching, in 400 yards or so, the edge of a wood (Roughtor Plantation). From this corner make direct for the height of Sheepstor—due west—but avoid climbing over any walls. In parts, they have already been demolished and can be negotiated without disrupting the stonework.

If you feel that your day is complete without sheep, walk south-west from the corner of the forest and turn left, on meeting the leat, and arrive at the Eylesbarrow Mine track near the end of the road. Otherwise, continue west to climb Sheepstor and enjoy the views (565682).

From this height, walk east to the bend in the leat and follow the water back to the starting-point at the end of the made-up road.

You have your collection of animals so, without waiting for quarantine restrictions, go home and annoy your friends with tales of your safari.

ITINERARY

	Accumulative Distance		Grid Refs
	km	(miles)	
Burcombe Gate			577673
Hen Tor	3.0	(1.75)	594653
Hart Tors	6.0	(3.75)	603675
Calves Lake	6.5	(4.0)	608676
Great Gnats Head	7.5	(4.75)	617679
Ducks' Pool	8.25	(5.0)	628678
(Fish Lake)*	10.25	(6.5)	647681
Fox Tor	13.25	(8.25)	626699
Crane Hill	14.0	(8.75)	sq. 62-69
Cuckoo Rock	17.75	(11.0)	585687
Sheepstor	20.75	(13.0)	565682
Car Park	23.5	(14.75)	577673

*2.5 km less (1.5 miles) if omitting Fish Lake

9

Doing The Pools
A Walk to Draw you Away from Home

From the moor-gate near Harford (643595) is a walk which will take you on a less-than-direct route to Princetown and will include views of many stretches of water. Harford is nearly 2½ miles north of Ivybridge (signposted from the Erme bridge) or 4 kilometres if you prefer. At Harford, where the church and picturesque bridge dominate the scene, turn right at another signpost which points to the moor. At the top of the hill, go through the gate to a well-used car park.

A locomotive on the old Redlake Railway

From here, walk on a bearing of 45° (north-east) for 1.75 km uphill to almost the top of the hill, crowned with cairns, and reach a broad track, nearly 3 metres wide running NNW-SSE. Turn left and follow the track for nearly 3 km. On the way, Sharp Tor will be passed 200 metres away on your left, and there is some fine scenery, also to your left, across the Erme valley to Stall Moor, crowned by Stalldon Barrow. On the barrow, a large turf-and-stone cairn, is Hillson's House which will be visited if you undertake the "Round the Houses" venture. In time, on the track, remains of railway buildings will be passed and, just before you have walked 3 km on

64

the track, Left Lake Pool appears on the right (647634). Left Lake itself is the stream running down the valley past many china-clay spoil heaps. The Pool has been flooded naturally, filling in a depression from which kaolin (decomposed felspar) was extracted. This particular area features in the latter part of Eden Phillpott's book, "Brunel's Tower", and the railway—which runs 12 km from near Bittaford to the former Redlake china clay works in the central southern moor—is the final scene of the hero's short life.

From this first pool, a tramp of 1½ km across some rough ground at 50° will lead you to Knattabarrow, a prominent "bump" on the horizon at the halfway stage. This feature serves as a guide to your next winner on the pools; walk from the barrow 350m on 310° to Knattabarrow Pool (655644). William Crossing likens this stretch of water to a tarn and believes it to be a natural phenomenon, but the several heaps around the water give some doubt to his assumption and suggest that the pool is a waterlogged peat-hag. The area around it is certainly desolate but easy to leave. From Knattabarrow Pool, keep on the same bearing of 310° and another 400m walk will bring you to the railtrack which you left at Left (of course) Lake. Turn right and, while taking in the wild nature of the upper Erme area, don't forget to look out for man's endeavours in this part of the moor. On the right, after 1 km and within 100m of the track, filter-beds for the clay works at Redlake will be seen. (Well worth a visit if you don't know anything about nineteenth century technology.) From this point the track veers to the right until it faces the direction it has come from, but, far from going in ever-decreasing circles and disappearing down its own claypit, it turns north again towards the larger green-grey pyramid. Keep on the track and when it terminates, continue in the same direction to meet a large pond (645669). This is the big brother of the Left Lake pond and, being man made, its depth is difficult to fathom. Suffice it to say that, during the drought of 1984, the South West Water Authority pumped water from this reservoir into the Avon valley at a rate of 150,000 gallons a day via the Henglake valley to the east.

Although a most interesting archaeological site, the pools mut be completed—I almost said "filled in"—so turn south west and walk toward the Redlake and Erme Valley, on the way passing some miry ground, then turn right along one of the narrow paths and walk west. Drylake is crossed first, its wide shallow valley showing many small tinners' heaps. In just under ½ km another south-bound

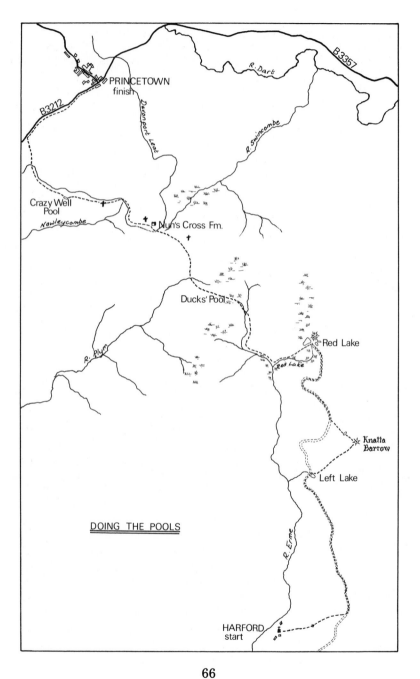

R. Dart

B3357

R. Swincombe

PRINCETOWN
finish

B3212

Devonport Leat

Crazy Well
Pool

Nawleycombe

Nun's Cross Fm.

Ducks' Pool

R. Plym

Red Lake

Red Lake

Knatta
Barrow

Left Lake

DOING THE POOLS

R. Erme

HARFORD
start

66

tributary will be met. This is the Blacklane Brook—according to the OS—or Wollake—according to the historian. Turn northwards and make your way upstream to the first major confluence, about 1¼ km from the Erme, where the remains of a blowing house can be seen on the spur of the two streams. From here, take a bearing of 330° and, after a short rise to gain higher ground, you will see a marshy area ahead of you in a wide depression. This is Ducks' Pool (628678), more of a pool than Cranmere, but only a pool after a great deal of rain. It is only a boggy waterhead, typical of nearly all Dartmoor rivers and streams. I've never seen any ducks here, but Sir Francis Drake's wife may have visited this spot while her husband surveyed the land nearby for his projected watercourse. Look for the largest boulders near the eastern bank of the fen, and before you meander off again look at the metal plaque affixed to the boulder. If I recite the inscription here, you may not need to look for the plate, but it evokes the memory of another lover of Dartmoor. The cubic structure next to it is the famous (or infamous) letterbox. The 1:25000 map of Buckfastleigh which you should all be looking at now has printed "Letter Box (memorial)" and as you will see, the two are related through this personality.

Moving on to the next port-of-call, avoid any boot-filling exercises by walking clockwise around the marsh from the letterbox, going north-west as soon as the marsh is behind you. The exact bearing is not vital so long as North Hessary Tor's TV mast is visible, as it will be towards this structure that you will walk for a couple of kilometres. Should the mast not be visible during your walk from Ducks' Pool, due north-west (315°) for the same distance will bring you towards your next pool. The first valley, here a wide basin, is the birth of the river which gives its name to the largest town in the South-West. (No, not Bristol or Gidleigh, but Plymouth.) If you have a day or three to spare, you are a seeker of variety in your life, and don't mind civilisation too much, a walk from here (Plym Head) to Plymouth is just for you. The slope up from the infant Plym, or, in a dry summer in its pre-natal stage, brings you between Eyles-barrow with its cairns to the west and the featureless Crane Hill. But as you walk, the vista before you expands, (*now* can you see the mast?). The head waters of Fox Tor Stream, Foxtor Mires, Nun's Cross Farm and Whiteworks (see the Abbot's Way walk) appear and you may be able to point out Devonport Leat contouring the opposite bank and bending west to disappear from view. As Nun's Cross is, as near as makes no difference, north-west from Ducks' Pool, no alteration of your compass is required. Make towards the Farm as this will be your next guide. If you need a break here, and want to decline the chance of going for the jackpot, walk north-west to the cross and follow the track north to Princetown 3 km away. Otherwise, please read on.

Face west from the farm, walk until you find yourself facing down a valley—about 250m—and dropping into the lower terrain pick up the leat as it emerges from the tunnel (602698). Make for the north bank and follow the water for another 3km. The first object of interest on this part of the walk is a modern cross inscribed "SLH" and a date which shows that the cross is by no means an antiquity. The valley of Newleycombe Lake stretches out to the left as the leat bends northwards, passing sluice-gates, then the track from Peat Cot, which crosses the leat by concrete sleepers, bearing west again, gives a view into Newleycombe. Walk now on the leat-side keeping above the track which runs parallel to it bending to the west and crossing two deep workings. Keep a lookout to your left and note one cross about 200m away and a second, one kilometre further on. Walk towards this cross and then from it, west again towards the

Where the Devonport Leat spectacularly meets the River Meavy

heaps. Behind them, and surprisingly some way below you, is the surface of Crazywell Pool (582704). The myth of the Walkhampton Church bell-ropes is retold in many books.

Regain the leat by walking north and crossing the water by the footbridge. Follow the leat north-west for another mile (1.5 km) to where it drops more quickly and eventually crosses the River Meavy by an iron aquaduct (573714). As the force of the water is so great, a diversion from the leat to the river has been created but, to compensate for this loss, there is a regulated flow from the Meavy into the leat. This runs through the large iron pipe clearly seen on the right of the river. The leat turns south and runs into the forest which surrounds Burrator Reservoir. Of the five million gallons a day borne by the Devonport leat, about one-third enters the reservoir by a spectacular waterfall near the road which runs north from the dam. The other two-thirds is fed into treatment works at Dousland between Princetown and Yelverton.

From the aquaduct, walk upstream keeping on the west bank of the river to a spot where, near a waterfall (Black Tor Falls), there are two blowing-houses, one on either side of the water. Above the falls, and avoiding any marshy area, you can follow the river upstream (about NNE) for another mile to Devil's Bridge, where the Plymouth-Princetown road is met. Tinners have been particularly active in this valley judging by the spoil heaps passed en route from the falls. Turn right and follow the road towards Princetown. If the ground north of Black Tor Falls is too wet and you decide that, at this stage of the walk, you will not be inconvenienced any further, bear north-west at any point, and in less than half-a-mile the road will be met, and follow it to the village.

One further pool can be looked for but today it is difficult to locate. Soldiers' Pond according to Crossing's Guide, is 200 yards before you come to the boundary of the Forest, marked by a stone on the right near the twin bungalows. It is on the right (south) of the road, but how far to the right is difficult to gauge as there are many hollows and water-filled pits between the road and South Hessary Tor, the prominent pile to the south-east.

Arriving, then, at Princetown, you may be able to "pool" your resources and have a meal at one of the cafes (if they're still open) or at one of the inns (if there is room). In the summer, the local bus company runs a service across the moor between Plymouth and Exeter but, with public transport, your routes are determined by

69

Princetown

time from beginning to end. Better perhaps to ask a friend to pick you up at a time which allows you enough rests to enjoy the walk more; better still, take bed and breakfast in Princetown and catch the mid-morning bus across the moor.

The pools *are* worth doing, but not every week!

ITINERARY

	Accumulative Distance		Grid Refs
	km	(miles)	
Harford—moorgate			643595
Left Lake Pool	5.0	(3.25)	647634
Knattabarrow Pool	7.0	(5.0)	655644
Redlake "Lake"	11.0	(7.0)	645669
Ducks' Pool	15.0	(9.25)	628678
Crazywell Pool	21.0	(13.0)	582704
(Soldiers' Pond)			
Princetown	26.0	(16.25)	591735

10

The Mariner's Way
(Goodbye, Sailor)

Historical Background

A couple of centuries ago, before the age of steam had caught up with sea-travel, it was possible, and indeed necessary, for a land-journey to take place. Sailors making for an embarkation at Bideford (or Dartmouth) might have been delayed by a variety of mis-fortunes: an ambush by footpads; too much ale the night before; an over-enthusiastic wife; or difficult conditions underfoot. Missing the boat at Bideford (or Dartmouth) meant an overland jaunt across Devon to catch the same vessel at Dartmouth (or Bideford). It occurred so frequently, by design or by accident, that the "Mariners' Way" became a well-used 80 mile path from coast to coast.

Unfortunately, very few records exist for most of the journey and the exact route, north of the A30 trunk road and south of Widecombe, is vague and contradictory. However, the section be-tween Widecombe and South Zeal or Firestone Cross, although arbitrary, is better documented. The National Park Committee and Devon County Council have erected many signs way-marking the "Way" across the eastern borders of Dartmoor, and it is almost certain that this was, in fact, the way of the late seafarers. As it is a linear walk, you may consider available means of transport at both ends. I found it better to start at Widecombe and walk north from that village, although it is barely adequately served by public trans-port in the summer.

From Widecombe, take the road north up the valley of the East Webburn, passing on the way Wooder Manor on the left, Bagpark, after a mile, and Isaford, past which a footpath leads ahead, be-tween the hedges, while the lane right-angles left. Just north of the Natsworthy estates a footpath approaches from the west (sign-posted) near an ancient boundary stone on the left-hand bank. This is inscribed "DS", which stands not for "ducking-stool" but "Duke of Somerset". Other examples of these stones can be seen on Hameldown Ridge at Single Barrow and Broad Barrow.

Here at Natsworthy Gate (721802), the footpath from Warren House via Grimspound crosses the lane en route to Jay's Grave and Manaton. The "Gate" refers to a former barrier across the road denoting the Natsworthy estate. It may have hung from the concrete posts on both sides of the road. The lane bends slightly to the right, but the "Way" goes through the smaller gate on the left and follows the sign pointing north: "Footpath to Moorgate on the B3212 Moreton Rd 2¾m". Fifty or so yards away is a stile leading into the wood and from now on you follow the yellow dots through two orange-spotted gates and enter a small pine wood.

Leapra Cross

The path emerges onto a field and then crosses a tarmaced bridle path. Here is another signpost pointing towards "Moorgate" which passes to the left of the thatched cottage "Heathercombe North", and skirts a field before entering a small pine wood. Four hundred yards on, the edge of the wood is reached and the fields around Kendon are bisected. Passing the farmhouse on your left, proceed north again when the farm-track angles east. An area of marshy ground is avoided as the "Way" cuts across three fields before turning left, and soon follows another farm track to Hookney.

Just where the made up lane goes right, between two farm buildings, turn left up a stony track for about seventy yards, turning right at the top, walking between moss-covered walls and under trees. In a few hundred paces the track bears left, rising slightly, but follow the "Footpath" sign to keep ahead before veering right. Continue for about 400 yards, crossing three fields and arriving at what may appear to be a dead-end at West Combe (709825). Here an intriguing right-of-way exists: it passes *through* an outbuilding (a cow-house a few months ago) and emerges at a cross-paths. Your route is straight ahead in front of the residences, but a fine example of an ash-house is found down your right hand path, built into the bank next to the track a little way down from the crossways. Continue for half-a-mile dropping gently to Moor Gate and Leapra Cross. The symbol itself is on the left hand bank as you approach a gate across your road. Although fairly short, its raised position makes it visible from the previous field gate.

Emerging onto the B3212 road at another sign-post (inscribed Mariners' Way) turn right, cross the road, and follow the direction indicated by another way-marked post to cross a stile. Bear slightly right to walk between gateposts, turn left and descend to a small stream, and bear slightly right continuing ahead between more gate-less gateposts. In less than half-a-mile from the road, you arrive at Lettaford (702840), a tiny settlement in the valley of the brook you have recently crossed. At the first junction of tracks turn right, then, still following directions from signposts, left along a walled track. The next few hundred yards are easy to negotiate— you cross Green Coombe Brook, a tributary of the River Bovey, and the lane from Chagford to the moor at Jurston. Here you turn left and almost immediately, right. The path here is fairly well defined and, approaching Lincombe, you meet another farm-track. Again a left-right movement will take you downhill to a footbridge over the North Wallabrook.

A made-up road is your companion now; it takes you south-west, yes, *away* from the destination. Being Mariners, the men would have realised this deviation but it is understandable if Hurston, the next hamlet, was a pub stop or overnight resting-place (686842). At the end of the road, follow the arrow right, along a straight path for 400 yards to Lower Shapley. The path turns left at this farmstead, only to turn right once again along the track for 200 yards, bearing left to edge two fields and enter the Chagford-Fernworthy road by steep steps in the wall. At this point, the Tom Cobley walk is encountered. Tom and his mates will be going home from the fair—should you

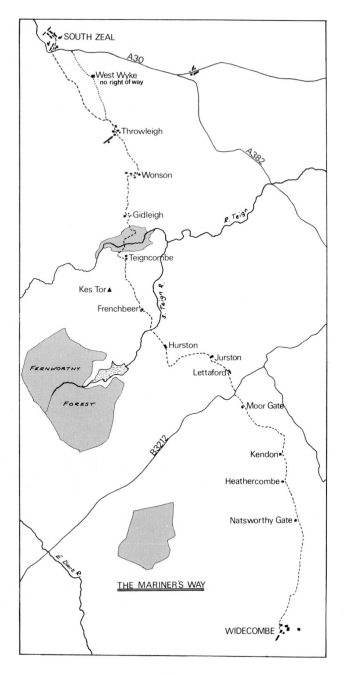

SOUTH ZEAL

A30

West Wyke
no right of way

Throwleigh

Wonson

Gidleigh

R. Teign

Teigncombe

Kes Tor ▲

S. Teign R.

Frenchbeer

Hurston

Jurston

Lettaford

FERNWORTHY

Moor Gate

FOREST

B3212

Kendon

Heathercombe

Natsworthy Gate

E. Dart R.

THE MARINER'S WAY

WIDECOMBE

meet them, help them on their way. They may be quite capable, or perhaps paralytic!

Again, few instructions are required as, at the time of writing, the way-marks and sign-posts are very helpful, showing not only the direction but many settlements for which to aim. Yardworthy, Teignworthy, Frenchbeer, Teigncombe and Gidleigh are inscribed on the arms of the signposts—some also give distance. You cross the South Teign river by a modern footbridge (678855) between the first two hamlets and the North Teign by another new contraption after Teigncombe (671875). (At this particular place, the lane is met with a farm on your right. Turn left, however, and in about 250 yards, right—almost due north.)

Emerging from the forested area, you are reminded of your route by a signpost pointing into the forest. Here, turn right and at the next tree-shrouded junction, left, pass the telephone box and, just before the little letterbox, go right, down a track to Gidleigh Mill (674887). Continue past the mill and at the next road turn left, cross the Moortown Brook and, just up the road, follow the sign to Providence Place. Emerge after a short, stiff uphill climb at a point just below the lemon-coloured chapel. Turn left here and go straight ahead at the signpost at Barrow Way Cross. Then turn off to the right at the sign which warns you to get out of your car as the route is not suitable. This is the same "Deave Lane" met on the Spreyton-Widecombe walk, via the grey mare.

It enters Throwleigh after a mile, opposite the church (688908). "Mariners' Way" is inscribed again on the sign at the bottom of the steps opposite Deave Lane. Climb these steps and go through a little iron gate into the churchyard. Keep to the path and meet the wall of the church at its north-west corner. Continue straight and leave the churchyard by a metal kissing-gate. Look ahead for a new stile, which you cross, and walk past the two very large trees in the same line. As you drop down, bear right but at the holly tree on your left, turn left. There is a less-than prominent "path" sign on your right. The faded orange blobs are with you again—you saw them on the trees just now, didn't you? Cross the brook and go uphill to the hedge, and follow the edge of the next two fields to enter another road (South Zeal to Throwleigh).

As on one or two other Walks in this book, the last part of the journey is the least satisfying. For easy instructions, and for a

South Zeal—Hello Sailors?

"light at the end of the tunnel" view, you may become relaxed, but for those who prefer grass under the feet, sorry!

If the Mariners' Way ever went to South Zeal—highly likely if the number of inns in the eighteenth century was the same as the number of inns here today—the way would have been via Moor View and West Wyke Farm. Unfortunately, there is no right of way and your only instruction, from the point at the end of the footpath (near Clannaborough Farm), is to walk north-north-west for the next two miles. To arrive at the centre of South Zeal, don't cross the main road (A30) but fork left and pass under it and continue ahead to the "Cawsand Beacon" inn (652936).

As I mentioned in the pre-amble to this walk, much of the exact way is unrecorded, but for a suitable finishing point, South Zeal will suit as it is just off the beaten track but accessible by whichever means of four- (or more-) wheeled transport you are catching.

ITINERARY

	Accumulative Distance		Grid Refs
	km	(miles)	
Widecombe			
Natsworthy Gate	4.5	(2.75)	721802
West Combe	8.0	(5.0)	709825
Lettaford	10.0	(6.25)	702840
Hurston	12.5	(7.75)	686842
South Teign	14.5	(9.0)	678855
North Teign	17.5	(11.0)	671875
Gidleigh	18.5	(11.75)	672884
Throwleigh	21.5	(13.75)	688908
South Zeal	25.5	(16.0)	652936

11

Round The Houses—North
(but via the wildest part of the moor)

Background Information

The habit of the Cornish to visit houses in a particularly noisy fashion on Floral Day can be re-enacted in Devon. Accompanied by their partners, the happy Helstonians dance through the front door and out of the back—and vice versa—of several homes in the streets of that quaint old Cornish Town. Without the music, and at a much less jaunty pace, this route undertakes to repeat the ritual through a few establishments on North Dartmoor.

Starting at Two Bridges (at the car park east of the road bridge—608750) walk north along the footpath towards Crockern Farm half-a-mile away. This house should *not* be visited uninvited as the occupants, like most Dartmoor farmers, lead a busy enough life without opening all doors for a succession of wayfarers. Instead, pass over a wall 250 yards away, veer right to gradually climb the slope, walking between the first "houses" of the day, and towards, eventually, the corner of the enclosure. There is a fallen part of the north wall in line with the tor ahead (Little Bee Tor—615769) and on the eastern wall, a gate. Make a little bee-line to the rocks and from here walk north a few hundred paces to Littaford Tor and, keeping in the same direction, Longford Tor (616779). Still gently ascending the ridge, keep to the left of the next and highest-situated tor, Higher White. In the wall ahead is another gate through which you pass and head, now descending, to Lower White Tor.

From here, you should be able to spot the next house to visit: Brown's House (615798) is just under half-a-mile away on a bearing of 325°. Don't expect a mansion, although Mr Brown *did* plan a fair-sized home. He is said to have been a peat-cutter but the quality of that fuel in this part of the morass is less than, for example, Amicombe Hill. On the way, the ground in the dip can be at best tacky but you have, at least, kept well away from the West Dart where the valley floor is always boggy.

Leaving Brown's House walk due north to a higher, more prominent wall and, turning right, follow it for 400 yards to its corner.

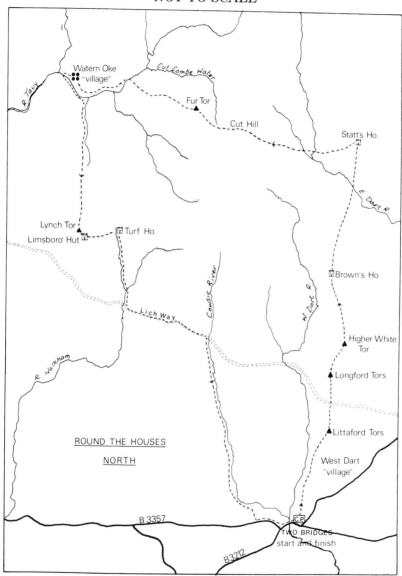

R. Tavy

Watern Oke
"village"

Cut Combe Water

Fur Tor

Cut Hill

Statt's Ho.

E Dart R.

Lynch Tor
Limsboro' Hut

Turf Ho.

Brown's Ho.

Cowsic River

N. Dart R.

Higher White
Tor

Lich Way

Longford Tors

R. Walkham

Littaford Tors

ROUND THE HOUSES

NORTH

West Dart
"village"

B 3357

C.P.

TWO BRIDGES
start and finish

B 3212

Walk north again, and in another 400 yards reach the eastern summit of Wildbanks Hill. Ahead of you, just over a mile away and on the highest part of Winney's Down, is Brown's next door neighbour (well, there *is* no-one else, is there?). You *can* make a bee-line for the house by setting your compass at 10° but there may be some difficulty met while crossing the East Dart river. Dry or easy crossing-places are scarce at the best of times but, being the intrepid journeymen and women that you are, a bootful is soon forgotten. In any case, once the Dart is overcome, just proceed uphill for half-a-mile and Statt's House (spelt with two or three 'T's) appears (621824).

A more substantial ruin this; the walls higher, the chimney-piece discernible and so too, the doorway. Don't bother to knock even though it may be occupied by fellow walkers. But please don't damage the walls and don't leave litter behind just because other less concerned people do; the dustbins aren't emptied weekly here! By now you have walked about five miles.

The next stage of your visitation takes you over the loneliest and bleakest part of Dartmoor, but it is nevertheless interesting, if not for the fine views on a clear day then for the compass-work required on a foggy one. Slightly north of west from Statt's House is Cut Hill, notable for two things: (i) the most remote point in England south of Northumberland's Pennines and (ii) the enormous amount of peat-cutting on and near the summit. Making for the highest part of the hill from Statt's House, the way leads downhill to the East Dart again where you will pass Kit Rocks on the east bank of that river. They consist of masses of granite, fairly tall but, being low, forming more of a cliff than a tor. Crossing the Dart and, 250 yards later, a long but unnamed tributary (both negotiated with comparative ease), climb the slope and arrive at the top of Cut Hill. This is marked by *two* range noticeboards either side of a low grassy cairn. Almost in the same direction but slightly to the north is the impressive Fur Tor (588831). It is just under a mile away if you follow the sheep/human track around the contour.

At a bearing of 295°, Hare Tor can be spotted through the mist or the glare; it makes an ideal marker for, as you walk downhill towards it, it remains visible over the right bank of the River Tavy for most of the time. The Tavy, in fact, rises just south of Cut Hill, doubling back on itself to act as a guide on your left, while Amicombe Brook approaches from your right. Just above their con-

Looking towards Watern Oak on the Tavy

fluence is Sandy Ford (the second!) which you should use if at all possible. Below this point, the Tavy becomes a good guide but lacking in co-operation for those needing to cross it. The only regularly safe fording-place is near Rattlebrook Foot where an 'eyot' helps out at an opportune moment. By definition an 'eyot' is a term applied to an island in the middle of a river (or lake).

From Sandy Ford, follow the Tavy downstream for half-a-mile slightly climbing as you do so. Walking due west from the ford will be equally accurate as you will find not one house, but a plethora of homes, all one imagines, unoccupied since the early Bronze Age (GR sq 56-83). Sixty huts stood on this hillside site according to R. H. Worth in "Dartmoor", but it would take too long to dance through all of them, let alone find all of them. By this time, the less fit will begin to think about making tracks for the car and a rest. So leaving this, the Watern Oke Wimpey estate, walk downstream to the river-island, previously mentioned, to cross the river. Walk up the left (south-west) bank for half-a-mile to the Inner Redlake, a tributary gorging into the parent river from the south. Here, there is a small

The Rattle Brook

granite pillar denoting the limit of the Willsworthy Military Range; the familiar red-and-white range poles are also with you and these you follow up the Redlake. Another WD stone can be seen close to the water and this one will act as a sign for you to keep above the stream on the west bank to avoid the worst of the going. Due south, the rocks contributing to Lynch Tor will emerge (two miles from the confluence of the Tavy and Redlake). The terrain as you head towards them is rough. The two rutted tracks that you cross on the way were used as safer routes across this wilderness, from relative civilisation at Wapsworthy, to utter desolation at the Walkham Head peat workings.

At Lynch Tor, or rather Limsboro (566805) the cairn to the south of the granite piles, the ruins of the next house can be visited. This was the abode of a shepherd—he would have enjoyed the unbroken 360° vista but may have had trouble locating his woolly charges among the dips and gullies. From the cairn, walk due east and meet again one of the peat tracks you recently crossed. Follow it downhill to the River Walkham and, where it fords that water, go upstream for about 350 yards. A stream (but hardly deserving the name) enters the Walkham from the north and here is seen number four in your house-hunting. Called "Turf House" (574810) it is located by two granite pillars. "Turf" in moorman's language is peat and this erection once housed some of the fuel dug from the Walkham Head area.

Retrace your steps to follow the Walkham down river for half-a-mile or so to Sandy Ford the Third where the Lich Way (q.v.) crosses it. Bear left, and on a bearing of 115° follow the track into the Cowsic valley. The large white pole on the far bank is 130 yards above Traveller's Ford (591786) where you don't cross. Instead, walk south down the valley, preferably avoiding the marsh on the valley floor by keeping to the right bank. In one-and-a-half miles, and a little way below a fence and wooden footbridge, a weir indicates the junction of the Devonport Leat and the Cowsic. A walk along the bank of the leat will ensure firm, level ground for the next two miles until the main road (B3357) west of Two Bridges is met. The last house on this tramp may well be the "Free" one on the opposite bank of the West Dart. The car park is on the other side of the road from the hotel.

ITINERARY

	Accumulative Distance		Grid Refs
	km	(miles)	
Two Bridges			608750
West Dart "village"	1	(0.75)	612760
Brown's House	5	(3.0)	615798
Statt's House	8	(5.0)	621824
Watern Oke	14	(8.75)	sq 56-83
Limsboro' Hut	20	(12.5)	566805
Turf House	21	(13.0)	574810
Two Bridges	36	(22.5)	608750

12

Round The Houses—South
A circular walk!

Beginning at Harford moorgate (643595—for directions, see "Doing the Pools"—south), walk uphill due north-east to arrive just over a mile away at the track of the former peat railway. From near the top of this hill, Piles, the large cairns on Three Barrows are conspicuous, one mile away, due north. Make for these, either by way of the track before veering right to climb steeply uphill, or by walking across the grass in a direct line to the top of the hill. From the triangulation pillar near the south-eastern "barrow" take a bearing of 25° and head that way for three-quarters-of-a-mile to the valley of Middle Brook. From Three Barrows, Eastern Whitebarrow is seen on a clear day, two miles away on 30°, in which direction it is also possible to travel, but it will bring you lower down the brook. On the way, and at about half-way, the valley of the Redbrook falls away to your right. Walk up the Middle Brook valley to the ruins of Uncle Ab's House (657637).

The remains of the building are less impressive than those at Bleak House on the Rattlebrook, although these have been untouched by fire power from military exercises. Who Uncle Ab was is not certain, but he could have well been the ostler who kept the Zeal Tor Tramway supplied with sound horses from the stables, above which he slept. The "Track of Old Tramway", as the OS depicts, is joined by the "Jobber's Path" which curved around the head of Middle Brook. It is feasible that jobbers, too, and their beasts of burden could both take a well-earned rest at this house, with Ab putting up the horses for the night in the shelter of this valley.

Climbing out of the valley, up the eastern bank ahead to the north rises Knattabarrow, a prominent object in this area of flat uninviting marsh. This ancient pile is noted on the "Doing the Pools" route and once again its eminence can be used as a guide towards your next visit. From here, both Eastern Whittaburrow (looking less like a submarine from this angle than from the Abbot's Way) and Western Whitebarrow are prominent on the near horizon. (Both spellings and pronunciations are acceptable.) No bearings are necessary, but instead watch your step as you trudge towards the latter. The head of Bala Brook is passed on your right in less than half-a-mile and, soon after, the clear, grassy track of the Zeal Tor tramway is met. This path leads directly to the barrow itself (653655). Easily distinguishable among the rocks, and close to the stump of a former cross are the remnants of a small house. It was reputed to be the weekday hostel for workers at Redlake china-clay works, but why anyone should want to spend five or six nights in such an exposed spot is hard to fathom. They did, however, have enough ready-to-hand building material, and they even broke off part of the cross to act as a lintel for the doorway. The cross, incidentally, was not connected with any religious function, but one of a number erected by Sir William Petre, who lived in the seventeenth century at Brentmoor House, above Shipley Bridge. The only other bondstone which signified the edge of his estate is down the hill from Whitebarrow and is called "Huntingdon Cross", which is passed on the Abbot's Way.

Leaving this, the high-spot of this walk, go due west for one mile. You cross, once again, the Redlake track, a row of boundary stones—Harford parish on the west, Ugborough on the east—and

Brent Moor House, before it was demolished, on the road from Shipley Bridge to the Avon Dam

arrive, as the ground dips more sharply away from you, at more houses, or to be precise, huts. There are three large enclosures in the vicinity, the most well-known being the most northerly, Erme Pound (639656). The huts, or rather the ruins of the circular houses, are found near the river at the northern wall of the enclosure. R. H. Worth gives a full account of the archaeological significance of Erme Pound in "Dartmoor", pp 102, 203-204. Moving south to the next two enclosures, with the Erme on your right, approach the next valley where a stream runs west. This is Hook Lake, and near its confluence with the Erme, set into the south-facing bank, is a blowing-house (639651). It is a fine example of those used by tinners to refine cassiterite "in situ". Power to move the stamps to crush the ore was obtained, like the majority of blowing-houses, by taking water from the river by way of a leat and feeding it onto a water-wheel. The leat can still be followed from the Erme and the water-wheel pit seen. Counting this as another "house" for your collection, cross the Erme as soon as possible, as this river, like the Tavy and some reaches of the Dart, does not make negotiation easy.

One mile below Hook Lake, and flowing into the Erme from the north-west, is Blatchford Brook; no trouble should be had in crossing this tributary. Half-a-mile below this brook, a weir has been built across the Erme and has vehicular access by way of a track on the west bank. Less than three hundred yards below this, a small stream emerges from a small defile and, at the eastern end of this little gorge, a grass-and-heather-covered mound is encountered. Facing upstream (west) is an entrance, giving rise to speculation as to its function. Although one of its names is Downing's House, I have failed to find any reference to anyone of that name in this connection. It is also known as Smuggler's Hole with obvious reasons, but as the Erme is replete with reminders of tinners' activities from Erme Pits downwards, it was probably made to be used as a cache for their implements (639629).

One more call to make—to the house of Hillsdon—and it is very easy to get to and find: uphill all the way (200° from Downing's House). The large cairn on top of Stall Moor (637623) gives wonderful views all around especially if it is not foggy! To the east and north-east are those places visited earlier on this trek—Three Barrows, just north of east; Western Whitebarrows at 30°; and to the south-east Piles Hill. On the northern slope of this cairn can be distinguished four low walls among the stones. A legend which

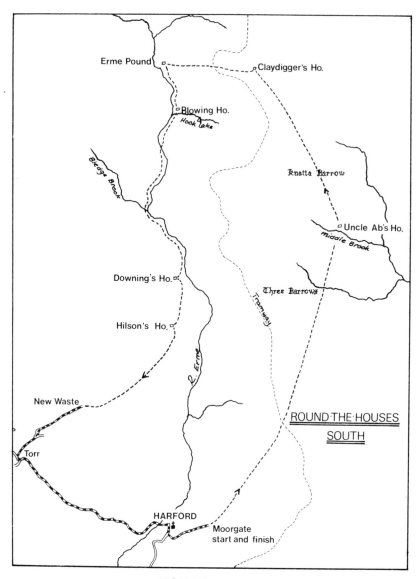

Erme Pound

Claydigger's Ho.

Blowing Ho.

Hook Lake

Knatta Barrow

Bledge Brook

Uncle Ab's Ho.

Middle Brook

Downing's Ho.

Three Barrows

Tramway

Hilson's Ho.

R. Erme

New Waste

ROUND·THE·HOUSES

SOUTH

Torr

HARFORD

Moorgate
start and finish

NOT TO SCALE

87

Crossing remarks upon is that an infant boy was abandoned on this moor, found by and subsequently brought up by a couple living in the vicinity. The obvious name to give him was applied: "Son of the Hill". Leave this hill on a bearing of 230° and walk for over three-quarters-of-a-mile to a gate in the wall, to the *right* of the building with a light-covered roof. As this is private property (SWWA) don't enter through the gate to the left of the building, although it is easier to reach the lane-end at New Waste.

Passing through the gate, follow the next wall under the trees to the left and approach the small car park and gate where the concrete track leading from the SWWA office joins your way. Unfortunately, the rest of the walk is on adopted lanes but it is easy to find the way back to the car. Short cuts from Stall Moor are not advised. First, there is the Erme to re-cross which is practically impossible to do without wading. Then, there are several enclosures on both sides of the river to avoid. None of them constitute "common land" complete with helpful stiles, signs and waymarks. Third, the slope both to and from the river is very steep and therefore more dangerous and even steeper than that from the church to the moorgate.

Therefore, from New Waste (625611) walk downhill for half-a-mile to turn left at the first junction and left again immediately (signposted "Harford"). In about one-and-a-half miles the bridge is crossed, then the church is met, beyond which you turn left uphill back to the moorgate and your car. Talk about "Avon Calling", more like "Erme"—who'd be an Avon lady on this round?—nobody's in.

ITINERARY

	Accumulative Distance		Grid Refs
	km	(miles)	
Harford—moorgate			643595
Uncle Ab's House	5.0	(3.0)	657637
Western Whitebarrow	7.0	(4.25)	653655
Erme Pond	9.0	(5.50)	639656
Hooklake Blowing House	9.5	(5.75)	639651
Downing's House	12.0	(7.75)	639629
Hillson's House	13.0	(8.50)	637623
Harford	19.0	(12.25)	643595

13

The 1984 "Dartmoor 100"

Background Information

Every year since 1973, the Long Distance Walkers' Association invites its regional groups, in turn, to set a route covering a hundred miles over and around its respective backyards. After visiting Snowdonia, the Weald and Lakeland in past years, the Association suggested a return to the south-west and "invited" the Cornwall and Devon group to prepare a walk on Dartmoor for 1984. Before and while planning such a route, special considerations have to be taken into account.

SIZE OF ENTRY: Typically, LDWA 100s attract over three hundred walkers (or rather participants, as a few prefer to jog the course). The event is walked non-stop with an upper time-limit of forty-eight hours for completion. By "non-stop", it is meant that a sit-down snack is available at checkpoints, but there are no facilities for sleeping, nor even for forty winks. Most walkers spend only one night out and the earliest arrivals finish in somewhat over twenty hours. In the past, about one-third of the entrants drop out and fail to complete the course.

CARE OF PARTICIPANTS: An extensive organisation is required to "process" the walkers before the start, support them during the event, care for early retirements and to receive walkers at the finish. The locality dictates either a circular or a linear walk— walkers and organisers prefer a circular route.

AVAILABILITY OF HEADQUARTERS: The start and finish must be readily available by public transport, have adequate over-night accommodation for early arrivals, and parking space where several vehicles can be left safely for forty-eight hours or more. The administrative advantages of having start, operational control during the event, and finish all in one site are many. Tavistock proved an ideal location for 1984's event, the LDWA having use of the army barracks in that town.

SITING OF CHECKPOINTS: Walkers pass through a series of checkpoints which fulfil a dual role: providing support such as food and drink, medical aid, and, very important psychologically, encouragement to the participants. The checkpoints also ensure admin-

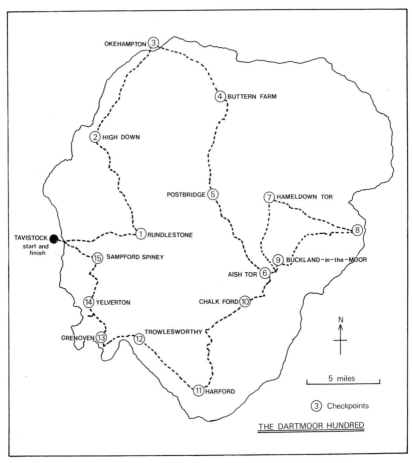

NOT TO SCALE

istrative control with radio links between successive points and with headquarters. All checkpoints need to be accessible by vehicle and have running water at hand. Spacing of checkpoints follows a well-proven formula, becoming closer together in the later stages of the route where walkers can be expected to be tired. Finally, the official route between checkpoints are the shortest in terms of time and/or distance, so as to discourage walkers to think of short cuts. The choice of route, therefore, is influenced by the availability of suitable checkpoints. A good example of the influence exerted by these particular considerations on the choice of route is the apparent deviation off the moor, but still in the National Park, to Liverton. This was because Liverton's village hall possesses the full facilities required for a midway breakfast stop.

ROUTE AND TERRAIN: It was decided that difficult sections would be covered during daylight and, if possible, route-finding during the night would be more straightforward. With a 10 am start, most walkers on the "Dartmoor 100" would have reached Postbridge (38 miles) by nightfall. During the night, their route would be mainly on well-defined tracks and friendly country roads, (the type where the middle is marked by grass rather than white lines!). Limited use of roads is allowed, even welcomed by many walkers, but busy main roads are avoided, especially where walkers are likely to be tired.

AESTHETICS: The route was planned to be visually pleasant, varied and challenging, the challenge being part cross-country and involving 12,000 feet of climbing. This includes Cosdon Hill from Belstone and, after eighty miles, Penn Beacon from Rook, 800 feet in one-and-a-half miles.

ACCESS: Finally the route has necessarily to be over public rights of way or tracks where public access is usually enjoyed. This involves close co-operation with National Park Authorities and landowners. The organisers enjoyed extensive goodwill from all concerned in this vital area of route-planning.

It is then, with the most kind permission of Tony Redfern of Plymouth, that the exact route is reproduced. Tony, along with Don Allen, Sue Coles and many others, walked and checked and checked and walked again each part from checkpoint to checkpoint and inserted major and minor deviations to necessitate a total of 100 miles. Apart from walking from Checkpoint 1 to 3 and 6 to 9 beforehand, and from 11 to 13 as a sweeper, my role was passive but repeatable. For a change, I *watched* the participants trot, stumble, march, crawl or limp in and out of a well-appointed checkpoint near Shaugh Bridge.

CHECKPOINT DETAIL

No.	Location	Between CPs km	(miles)	Accumulative miles	CP Open from	to
Start	Tavistock					
1	Rundlestone	9.3	(5¾)	5¾	11.00	12.45
2	High Down	16.2	(10¼)	16	13.00	18.15
3	Okehampton	12.6	(7¾)	23¾	14.30	21.15
4	Buttern Farm	10.5	(6¾)	30½	16.00	00.30
5	Postbridge	12.7	(7¾)	38¼	18.00	04.00
6	Aish Tor	11.7	(7¼)	45½	19.30	07.30
7	Hameldown	11.6	(7¼)	52¾	21.30	11.00
8	Liverton	11.9	(7½)	60¼	23.30	14.30
9	Buckland	12.0	(7½)	67¾	01.15	18.00
10	Chalk Ford	7.4	(4¾)	72½	02.30	20.00
10a	Huntingdon	(3.1)			03.15	21.00
11	Harford	11.9	(7¾)	80¼	04.30	24.00
12	Trowlesworthy	10.8	(6¾)	87	06.30	03.00
13	Grenoven	3.9	(2½)	89½	07.15	04.00
14	Yelverton	6.4	(4)	93½	08.30	07.30
15	Sampford	5.5	(3¼)	96¾	09.15	09.00
16	Tavistock	6.2	(3¾)	100		10.00

ROUTE INSTRUCTIONS

KEY

rd	road	fb	footbridge	RH	right hand
fp	footpath	br or Br	bridge	LH	left hand
bp	bridlepath	x or X	cross	TR	turn right
r or R	river	M	miles	TL	turn right
tk	track	R	right	FR	fork right
km	kilometres	L	left	FL	fork left
m	metres				

N, S, E, W   general direction
080′ wds, 260′ wds   approx compass bearing

"A view across the valley of the
moorland Lyd towards Brent Tor"

Start (GR 493739) to CP1 (Rundlestone)

Take Whitchurch Down/Princetown rd E keeping to LH verge. After 2.2 km TL at Warren's X. Continue N on rd for 350m when TR along rd to E.

At Moortown, reached after 1.3 km, when rd turns 90°R continue uphill 080'wds over open moor to cross leat, after 900m by stone cross.

Continue downhill 080'wds, keeping on a line L of Vixen Tor, and from valley bottom uphill 040'wds to reach B3357 after 1.35km. At rd TR and continue along verge for 3.2 km to reach CP1 (Rundlestone) (GR 575750).

CP1 to CP2 (High Down)

Take B3357 E. After 300m TL thru' gate and follow clear tk N to reach barn after 900m. Continue N on tk to reach mesh fence after 950m.

Pass thru' gate and TL uphill (fence on L) to reach Prison Leat in 200m. At leat TR and continue upstream with leat on L. After about 1.1 km cross to opposite bank (plank in place 1983), continue upstream to reach, in about 400m, small marker post (no 7) at edge of leat. Continue N for 150m to reach stone leat overflow, where BL 300° across rough ground to reach after 250m R Walkham.

Cross river at 'ford' to pick up clear sunken tk 240'wds on far bank. Tk soon bears round 280'wds and becomes indistinct in places. After 2.4 km reach a conspicuous standing stone.

From standing stone 310° to reach and follow wall on R. When

93

wall turns N (700m from standing stone) head 330° downhill over open moor. After 850m, reach gate in walls merging from L and R.

Thru' gate and on waymarked path N to reach rd at Wapsworthy after 350m. TL along rd, after 500m TR at rd junct, continue N, cross R Tavy at Hill Br and reach after 1.5 km fork in rd. FL (signposted to Mary Tavy) and when rd turns 90°L, after 500m, thru' gate and tk uphill 310'wds.

Pass thru' second gate, after 200m, and where tks divide take RH tk 350°. Keep on 350° across open moor shortly to reach grassy tk and continue 350'wds to reach, after 1.1 km, small building by leat. Cross leat on tk 310° to reach second small leat after 100m, TR follow leat on L to reach rd after 550m. Head 040° over open moor to rejoin leat on L after 900m. Follow line of red/white range marker posts 050'wds to reach, after 500m, the first marker on far bank of leat.

Cross leat and head 020° towards conspic trees. Cross Walla Brook and continue with old farm walls on L to reach Doetor Brook after 900m. TL downstream and cross to RH bank at first opportunity to reach tk, by br on L, after 150m. Take tk R uphill,

Footbridge over the River Lyd at High Down

The King Way on the Dartmoor 100

350'wds, to cross R Lyd by fb and reach CP2 (High Down) (531857) after 750m.

CP2 to CP3 (Okehampton)

Recross fb and follow E bank of R Lyd N to reach, after 700m, ford (at point where wall on far bank turns uphill). Cross ford and with wall on L uphill for 150m to TR along old tramway.

Continue N along tramway for 3 km to where it ends in a "roundabout". FL to join, after 200m, tk N, passing Sourton Tors away to L after 1 km.

Continue 020'wds downhill on broad grassy tk to reach gate in wall, after 850m. Thru' gate, follow bp N between walls for 700m to reach gate. Thru' gate, then 065° over South Down (signposted to Meldon Reservoir) to reach Meldon Dam after 1 km.

Thru' gates, cross rd (dam on R) along bp (signposted to Meldon Viaduct) with wall on L for 300m. 20m after wall bears sharply L, BR thru' gap in wall ahead, then downhill on watery/muddy tk to rejoin bp in 100m. Continue with W Okement river on R for 100m to reach fb. Cross river, TL and continue with river on L, thru' quarry gate to reach rd after 350m.

TL along rd, under viaduct, and after 1 km (just past corrugated iron bldgs on R) FR on tk off rd, thru' iron gate, after further 50m, then follow tk NE to reach golf course after 950m. Cross golf course on distinct tk, to join rd just past club house after 650m.

Continue NE along rd to join, after 850m, Tors Rd. TL downhill to reach CP3 at Tenby House after 650m (588951).

CP3 to CP4 (Buttern Farm)

Follow route on inset plan 350m to mill steps. At top of steps TR, then with mill leat on L and school on R along tk E, thru' 3 kissing gates, and Ball Hill woods, to reach T junct after 1.4 km. At junct TL uphill, shortly to join rd, and TR under railway br after 150m.

Continue E along rd for 350m when TR on fp (signposted to Cleave House) 150'wds over fb and stiles uphill to join rd after 800m. At rd TR, cross cattle grid, along rd to reach Belstone after 1 km.

In Belstone TR by Telegraph Office, pass Inn on your R, and at T junct on rd straight on to join clear tk downhill reaching River Taw after 300m. Cross river by fb (to R of ford) then 130° uphill over open moor to reach small stone row after 2.8 km.

From stone row 160'wds 1.2 km to cross Blackstone Brook by ford (647905), then 120'wds, keeping valley bottom to R and reaching rd by Shilstone Tor after 1.25 km.

At rd TR and continue S reaching tk to R after 600m, along tk to CP4—Buttern Farm (657894) after 250m.

CP4 to CP5 (Postbridge)

Take sunken tk S to reach open moor after 300m. Continue 195° to pass small walled field on R after 600m. DO NOT CLIMB ANY WALL. Continue 195° to reach Scorhill Circle after 1.25 km.

From Circle BL to cross leat by stone slab after 100m, then BR along tk to cross Wallabrook by clapper br after 200m. TL along brook to reach Teign-ever-Clapper in 100m, cross br to S. Head 180° over open moor for 700m, (marshy ground to R) then 210° for 1.3km to reach Fernworthy Forest.

Keeping Forest on L pass thru' gate in wall (just short of forest) and head SW, with forest close to L, for 1 km, when just after line of forest bears L pass thru' gate in second wall. Continue on clear tk 210'wds for 700m to reach gateway in third wall, then take clear tk

Near Teign-e-ver Clapper

S to reach a fourth wall after 800m. Pass thru' gate and in 150m reach Grey Wethers.

Follow clear tk S, crossing, after 1.35 km, a small stream coming down from R, and continuing on tk S to reach, in 800m, E Dart river from R joining stream on your L. Cross stream to E bank. Continue S downstream (good route on high ground to E of Dart) for 2 km, to reach a small fir copse.

Enter copse by small gate by river bank, continue SE along tk to reach open field after 200m, path is L along two sides of field, emerging on main rd (B3212) after 700m. TL along rd to reach CP5 (Postbridge Hall—652792) on R after 400m.

CP5 to CP6 (Aish Tor)

Retrace your steps SW along B3212, and immediately after crossing br, in 500m, TL thru' gate on bp, to reach second gate after 150m, thru' gate then sharp uphill and S along bp to join rd after 850m. TL along rd to reach cattle grid after 700m, where TL and with wall on L, E to Bellever Br after 300m.

Cross br TR, continue S with river on R, reaching plantation after 1.1 km. Thru' plantation close by river bank, to emerge after 700m,

97

at bp signposted to Sherril. TL on bp thru' gate and uphill SE, soon with wall on R and reaching a gate after 400m, thru' gate and continue on tk, between walls, SE to reach Babeny Farm (pse be quiet by night) after 750m.

Thru' farm to reach rd, continue on rd E and then S to reach minor x rds after 2.4 km, TR to reach main rd (B3357) after 150m.

Cross rd walk S with wall on L, swinging to 120° following line of wall. After 600m wall swings N, but continue on 120°, avoiding wet ground on L, to reach rd after further 100m.

TL along rd for 250m, when wall on R bears R away from rd. Follow line of wall along tk for 300m, when 2nd wall funnels in from L. Continue between walls to emerge, after 270m, on a heading of 205°.

Continue on tk S for 230m, when tk turns SE along a contour above R Dart. Remain on tk for 1.2 km, when tk is on heading 180°, TL along tk with wall on L, to reach CP6 (707715) after 600m.

CP6 to CP7 (Hameldown)

Continue E along tk to reach rd after 50m. TR along main rd and, after 200m, TL along tk with wall on L to reach Leigh Tor after 150m. Stay on tk, skirting Tor to your R, continue downhill to reach rd after 600m.

At rd, TL, and after 250m, FL uphill on rd to Lower Town. Pass Lower Town church after 2.0 km, and continue W on rd, to reach Ponsworthy 'Splash' after a further 1.2 km.

Cross shallow ford in rd, and take fp to R of cottage, N with W Webburn River on your R. After 1.2 km reach Jordan Mill. Cross fb, pass Mill, (pse be quiet by night) to reach rd where TR uphill 025'wds, over x rds, to reach a 2nd x rds after 1.1 km.

Leave rd on 025° over open moor, to join, after 1 km, tk coming in from R. Follow tk N, climbing gently. At Single Barrow, after 2.7 km, tk divides. Take LH tk 340'wds to reach CP7—Hameldown Tor—(703806) after 1.1 km.

CP7 to CP8 (Liverton)

From CP7 090° across open moor for 500m, to join clear downhill tk. Follow tk E to reach, after 1.3 km, Natsworthy Gate.

½L across rd to join bp E, and reach rd at Jay's Grave after 1.2 km. TR follow rd SE 1 km to Swallerton Gate. From Swallerton uphill on 120° to pass between main granite outcrops of Hound Tor

More intrepid Hikers at Jay's Grave

after 400m. Continue 120'wds downhill to reach, after 300m, remains of medieval village. Skirt L of village 100'wds, reaching, after 200m, a gate.

Thru' gate (signposted Leighon) continue on bp downhill to cross brook by stone br after 400m. Thru' rickety gate then uphill on clear path thru' woods. At signpost to Leighon, reached after 300m, continue uphill 100'wds (ignoring tks forking off R) and swinging round to 150° just before reaching crest of hill, after 450m. Continue 150° for a further 150m, when TL onto 120°.

Continue 120'wds, soon tk becomes well defined and reaches rd by spot ht 362m after 1.1 km. Cross rd and continue 120'wds on clear tk (ignoring tk forking R just after crossing rd), to join a further rd after 1.0 km.

TL along rd and after 70m FR down rd (signposted Green Lane). Remain on rd ESE to reach T junct after 1.7 km. Straight on, along tk between banks for 1.0 km when surface becomes metalled. After a further 100m TR on tk 160° between hedges, to reach, after 500m, T junct by thatched cottages. TR, and in 60m TL along rd, keeping L at fork, to reach CP8 (Liverton Village Hall) on L after 200m (806752).

CP8 to CP9 (Buckland)

TR, return NW along rd, towards Ilsington for 1.6 km, when, just

99

after crossing small bridge, FL on rd up steep hill. Reach Ilsington and pass pub on R after 850m, straight on, over staggered x rds 250'wds to reach Methodist Ch on L after 750m, continue 250'wds for a further 500m to reach Birchanger X.

At X TR towards Haytor, and after 200m, (at RH bend in rd) leave rd and keep straight on down tk 350'wds into woods. Cross stream at bottom, then up winding tk to reach gate after 500m. Thru' gate, continue on tk between walls to reach open moor after 100m. Then join tk 260'wds and continue for 350m to reach 5 bar gate. TR before gate and follow wall on L for 1.6 km to just below Rippon Tor.

Continue uphill S (wall now 50m to your L) for 350m, to reach gap in wall, then W a further 250m to reach Rippon Tor, which pass on your R. Take tk downhil 220°, thru' gate in wall, keep on 220° to pick up clear tk downhill with remains of wall on R. Pass through gate in wire fence then 220°, over wall by marker, and reach rd by Cold East X after 1.15 km.

Follow rd S from Cold East X for 400m to reach cattle grid. TR before grid and follow line of wall on L uphill to Buckland Beacon, reached after 900m. (Stop at Beacon to look at 10 Commandment

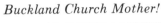

Buckland Church Mother!

100

Stone) continue downhill S on tk over rough ground, to reach clear path, and after 500m, join rd.

TR along rd, passing over br after 1.1 km, and TL on rd downhill after a further 400m, just before Buckland Church. Continue downhill for 100m to CP9 (720730).

CP9 to CP10 (Chalk Ford)

Continue downhill on rd, over Buckland Br, then on rd with R Dart on L to reach B3357 at Barren Corner after 2.35 km.

TL downhill along B3357, to cross Newbridge after 400m, and immediately over br TR over stile and follow fp towards Holne. Cross several more stiles and keeping to RH side of fields on fp reach rd after 1.3 km.

At rd TL, then TR down rd to Holne. At x rds, after 200m (Church House Inn on R) straight on towards Scorriton, to take, after a further 350m, tk on L downhill marked 'unsuitable for motors'. On reaching rd, after a further 600m, TR and in 100m, just over br, TR uphill on rd to reach Scorriton after a further 400m. TR at T junct, then TL up lane to W 'no thru' road for motor vehicles' to reach, after 1.7 km, CP10 (Chalk Ford—685681).

CP10 to CP11 (Harford)

Continue W down tk for 400m to cross R Mardle by fb. Take broad tk uphill immediately S of br, taking RH fork after some 100m, and continuing S uphill on tk. When tk becomes indistinct/confused, after about 500m, head 235° until a broad, green tk running E/W up from Lud Gate, is reached in a further 500m.

TR on tk and continue for 350m to top of rise, then 235° over open moor to reach Huntington X by bank of R Avon, after 1.5 km.

Take tk W, with R Avon to your L, for 750m to reach clapper br. Cross br to S side then straight uphill on tk 210°. On reaching crest, after 150m, continue 210° over open moor to reach old tramway after 1.2 km.

TL and continue S along tramway, passing Leftlake Mires Quarry (water filled) on L after 2.0 km. Keep S on tk and after 2.7 km (at S end of 600m stretch on heading of 170°, and by standing stone on R engraved 'U') FR on grassy tk 180°.

At next standing stone, after 300m, FR 225° easy going over open moor to reach CP11 (Harford—643596) after 1.75 km.

CP11 to CP12 (Trowlesworthy)

Follow rd W to reach Harford Ch after 500m. TR along rd, which makes a general WNW direction to reach Torr after a further 2.5 km.

From Torr continue on rd NW (ignoring rds to R and L after 300/400m) reaching Hele X after 650m, where TL along rd, continue W for 500m to reach T junct where TR uphill 345'wds. Cross shallow ford after 300m, then uphill between walls to reach open moor after a further 300m. Continue uphill 340°, for 1.6 km, to reach Penn Beacon.

From Penn Bn (trig point) head 310° over open moor, passing Higher Trowlesworthy Tor close to L after 2.6 km, and Little Trowlesworthy Tor on R after a further 200m. From Lit Trowlesworthy Tor head 290° downhill to reach fb over leat after 500m.

Cross leat, and keep on tk W, passing farm on L after 500m, keep on farm tk downhill, swinging round to S, and reaching CP12 (Trowlesworthy—564644) after 650m.

CP12 to CP13 (Grenoven)

Continue on tk W to reach rd after 300m. TR along rd and, after 700m, just before Cadover Br, TL along rd S, with R Plym to your R.

Continue to reach 'sheep' road sign, after 200m, where TR off rd, follow ditch for 60m to reach stile and waymarked fp. Cross stile,

A time to reflect at Trowlesworthy Tors

follow fp (pipe track) ignoring all diversions, SW above R Plym to reach, after 1.8 km, wire topped stone structure on your R. Take RH tk, to reach a gate after 100m.

Thru' gate, TR down tk and, after 50m, TR over a stile to follow fp downhill, first over field, then cross second stile and thru' woods to emerge at rd after 400m. TR along rd, crossing Shaugh Br after 200m, to reach, thru' small car park and gate on R, CP13 (Grenoven—533637) after a further 100m.

CP13 to CP14 (Yelverton)

Retrace steps to cross Shaugh Br after 100m. TL along river bank and cross R Plym by wooden fb after 50m. Follow wooden palings round to R to take rough 'paved' tk uphill E for 300m, and reach old tramway. TL and follow tk slightly downhill, (keeping to higher tk just past Dewerstone Cottage), and with R Meavy on your L reach rd, over stile, after 1.35 km.

TL on rd, immediately crossing br and over stone stile in RH parapet of br into field with R Meavy on your R. Follow fp N, river to your R, to reach Clearbrook Br after 1.3 km. Over ladder stile, ½L across rd to join fp to Yelverton. Continue N, taking path to L of Yeoland Ho after 1 km, to reach, thru' old kissing gate, rd after 500m. TL on rd, under rly br, TR and follow path uphill, passing two fields on your L, to reach gate after 400m. Thru' gate, over dry leat, TR and keep on rd NW. Follow rd over dry leat on L, cross cattle grid and reach main rd, A386, after 400m.

Cross rd ½L, in direction of Buckland Abbey (NT), cross cattle grid onto Roborough Down, after 50m. TR, passing rock outcrop on L and head 350° over old airfield to reach CP14 (Yelverton—514680) after 900m.

CP14 to CP15 (Sampford Spiney)

Continue 350° between gorse for 300m, when gorse becomes heavy. Find path to R, then on tk 350'wds. Tk soon becomes distinct and downhill. After 1 km reach T junct in tk and TR slightly uphill, NE, for 150m, to reach rd by double bend sign. TR down rd and at hairpin bend, after 220m, TL off rd down tk, to pass thru' small gate on R after 80m. Continue N, passing former rly stn on L and reaching main rd, A386, after 200m. Straight on across rd, TAKE GREAT CARE—FAST TRAFFIC, and N downhill along rd to cross R Walkham at Horrabridge after 400m.

Over br, TR uphill on rd towards Princetown. At Grimstone Manor Lodge, on L after 850m, TR over stile on waymarked fp NE, which after 200m turns briefly L by stone building, passes thru' gate, turns R and continues NE, thru' many gates/stiles, to reach CP15 (Sampford Spiney—533724) after 2.1 km. (CP is to W of church.)

CP15 to Finish (Crelake Barracks, Tavistock)

Continue NW along rd for 500m to reach T junct. TL, continue on rd W signposted Tavistock/Whitchurch Down to reach Warren's Cross after 1.9 km. Continue W (on reverse of outward route), to reach 'start psn' after 2.2 km. TL in front of golf club house, and follow inset plan to reach Crelake Barracks after 1.6 km (481738).

Postscript to the "100"

Of the 310 starters, 206 completed the whole route, officially put at 100¼ miles. The weather on the first day took its toll on the rest of the entrants, it being a day of heavy intermittent showers. The conditions improved during the first night (Sat/Sun) and only two bursts of rain were experienced by the walkers on the last third or so during Sunday. Only a few dropped out having completed 85 miles,

Tavistock—always a welcome sight!

104

the 206 finishers finding it more worthwhile to carry on at such a stage in the proceedings.

The first home, classified like the next three as a "runner", clocked-up a time of 20 hours 23 mins; all four took less than a day to "do" the hundred. About 150 finished inside 42 hours, arriving at Tavistock during the second night, while the last nine to complete the course did so with half an hour or less to spare, the time limit being 48 hours.

The importance of checking-in on organised walks such as these, or "challenge" walks, is emphasised by the fact that as far as the organisers of the "100" are concerned, seven people are still walking around the moor. They obviously failed to let anyone know of their intensions and were last heard of at Huntingdon Warren, or Harford. One gentleman checked in at Tavistock, set off with the three-hundred others, and has yet to check in at Rundlestone, less than six miles away. Marshals and sweepers can only assume that if you are "late" arriving at a checkpoint—and "late" being the operative word—you will have the courtesy to inform the organisers as soon as you find a phone. No-one minds drop-outs, so long as they make it known that's what they are!

14

The Ten Tors Expedition
— some personal observations

There are few finer sights on Dartmoor than that met on a Sunday in mid-May, when, from scores of miles away, figures become recognisable as they emerge around Row Tor, West Mill Tor, or from the direction of Oke Tor, to converge on Okehampton Camp in assorted gaits in one gate. This is the ultimate scene of the Ten Tors event. This expedition differs from the others in this book in many ways and, therefore, I class it not as a walk, but a challenge. However, you may ask, "Isn't a hundred-mile walk a challenge by the distance?" It is, but the first difference is that a camp-out is compulsory in this event whereas such a pause would disqualify participants in the "100".

The other challenge walks are "open", there is no age limit—common sense prevails in most cases. Seven- or seventy-year-olds are rarely met on the "North-South", but Ten Tors entrants are limited to the 14-19 age group.

Another difference, related indirectly to the above, is that this event is preceded by many "practices", and meetings of team managers. There is also a fixed number, six, to a team, and all entrants have to complete to ensure a "successful" team.

Lastly, the route, unlike the other walks is not repeated year after year. Indeed, hardly two years lapse without a change in the route. The planners have a time-consuming task in ensuring that each of the 400 teams do not follow each other in three bee-lines for a day and a half. Each team has its own route, and consequently is self-reliant in the field of navigation.

Having said that, the event is worth noting here, not only because it is held on Dartmoor and is a "long" event (35, 45 or 55 miles), but also it trains the youth of today in social awareness and tests their individual confidences to tackle longer one-day walks. A fifteen-year-old who completes 35 miles in twenty-four hours is capable of walking 27 miles in eight hours by the time he or she is eighteen (assuming the same level of fitness is maintained over those years).

In the twenty-five years of its existence, the event has increased

A typically triumphant but tired Ten Tors team!

in popularity so much that today teams are vetted and it is unusual
for a first-time applicant to be admitted. There may be drop-outs
but the notification at the earliest possible date does not always
give a team adequate time for preparation.

The organisers (Headquarters, South West District, Bulford
Camp, near Salisbury) do a magnificent job, not only on the day, but
months before and weeks after. Every checkpoint is in radio-contact
with Okehampton Camp, the start and finish, and every individual
is cared for throughout the event.

I have refrained from calling it a competition. There are medals
for *all* teams completing their respective routes inside thirty hours.
Unfortunately, there are two or three schools who make it a habit of
"coming first". They have been seen to pitch camp near the last
checkpoint so that they can arrive at the finish minutes after
"opening-time". This is not the idea of the event; I believe those
who *earn* their medals are the groups who use their navigatory skills
thoroughly for up to 30 hours over 55 miles coming home on Sunday

afternoon mentally rather than physically exhausted. I see no point whatsoever in groups belting around the moor for ten or eleven hours, sleeping for eight and arriving before any one is around to cheer them home. They are usually schools on Dartmoor's doorstep, which get to know each tor by name and have little need to navigate. Unfortunately, the local press tends to name the first group in each section to complete as if it is a marathon race. It is a challenge lasting the best of two days and a night, and I wonder what the consequences would be if one of those groups had a serious casualty to contend with half-way across the moor.

The twenty-fifth running (!) of the Ten Tors (1960-85) was commemorated by the production of a well-compiled booklet. Alan Stephens, in particular, wrote a potted history of the event and contributions included those from the army, team managers and participants who submitted diaries of their experiences. May the event be continued for at least another twenty-five years.

In the land of "animals" above the River Lyd.

Getting 'sidetracked' on the way to Jay's Grave on "The Dartmoor 100" route.

*The "joys" of long distance Dartmoor walking
in a lane near Cornwood.*

Wistman's Wood in the West Dart Valley—where long distance walkers fear to tread.

An ancient stone row in the Dartmoor heartland.

111

DIARY OF A DARTMOOR WALKER by Chips Barber

Diary of a Dartmoor Walker is a light-hearted book which includes many unusual strolls, rambles, excursions, expeditions, safaris, pilgrimages and explorations into all areas of the Dartmoor National Park. There is the Lich Way, or the way of the dead (and the dying!), the Abbot's Way, the North/South Crossing and even the Tom Cobley Walk. This 'diary' spans the four seasons to provide Dartmoor enthusiasts with a splendid portfolio of drawings, photographs and three-dimensional profiles that capture Dartmoor in a way that no other book has managed so far - and the walks are quite interesting too!

DIARY OF A DEVONSHIRE WALKER by Chips Barber

If you enjoy reading *Diary of a Dartmoor Walker*, then you are sure to enjoy the further adventures of Chips Barber with his assorted walking companions in *Diary of a Devonshire Walker*! The book contains eight Dartmoor walks from all parts of the moor and also features walks in the Haldon Hills, along the South Devon Coastline and in the Tamar Valley, all amply illustrated with many maps and photographs.

THE A TO Z OF DARTMOOR TORS by Terry Bound

This is a complete gazetteer to all of Dartmoor's many tors from the grandest mass to the smallest rockpile. No Dartmoor bookshelf would be complete without this unique reference book.

THE TEMPLER WAY by Derek Beavis

Derek Beavis has put together a first class guide to The Templer Way, one which gives you the option of following it in short, simple stages or, if you are person enough, one long safari. The story of the Haytor Granite Tramway and the Stover Canal are but two of many historic features along the route which are fully described. Packed with maps and some splendid photographs, this book is the perfect guide to the Templer Way.

TEN FAMILY WALKS ON DARTMOOR by Sally and Chips Barber

Like the title suggests, this book contains ten walks on Dartmoor suitable for the reasonably fit family who wants to 'get away from it all' for just a few hours. These sensible strolls are interesting, include clear but simple maps, and reveal the most beautiful parts of Dartmoor. The walks range from just a few miles up to about 6 or 7 miles in length and are presented in a light and easy-to-read style.

WEIRD & WONDERFUL DARTMOOR by Sally and Chips Barber

Packed with amusing anecdotes and stories, some stranger than fiction, that could only happen in a place like Dartmoor, you can read about many of the bizarre escape bids from Dartmoor Prison, how a rat set a mill alight, about a henpecked husband and a goose-pecked vicar, and Dartmoor's more exotic wildlife — llamas, crocodiles and elephants! You don't believe there are any of these on Dartmoor? Well read this little book and discover the truth!